Praise for *After Trauma: Lessons on Overcoming from a First Responder Turned Crisis Counselor*

"Rothrock skillfully weaves together insights from her experiences as a firefighter, educator, advocate, and counselor to present a thoughtful guide to overcoming self-blame, shame, and other common reactions to trauma. Part memoir and part practical self-help guide, featuring simple but powerful exercises, the book will inspire survivors to connect with their inner strength and resilience in order to reclaim control over their futures."

> —Karla Vermeulen, PhD, deputy director, Institute for Disaster Mental Health at SUNY New Paltz

"A riveting page-turner! Rothrock demonstrates the power of owning your own experiences."

> —Adrianne Ziyad, trustee at Women in Fire

"*After Trauma* shines a light on the darkness that trauma leaves behind and guides survivors through the tunnel of recovery in a sensitive, supportive manner. Realizing I was not alone in my nonlinear journey of trauma recovery gave me a sense of peace and a feeling of solidarity with other survivors."

> —Kelly Herron, co-founder of RunBuddy and featured in the Runner's World documentary, *Not Today*

"This is an enlightening and special book. *After Trauma* is both a poignant memoir and an educational guide to resilience. By centering the light on the survivor experience and recovery, Ali Rothrock teaches us about our incredible capacity to create change, to heal from trauma, and to make our communities safer when we speak up against injustice and share our story."

> —Kristina Froling, Virginia Tech shooting survivor, and founder of The Koshka Foundation for Safe Schools

"Ali Rothrock provides a poignant and practical approach to dealing with trauma, seeing it as an opportunity for growth. She has found the balance of engagement and insight that reinforces the message that trauma is not the end of a journey but just the beginning."

—Sara Jahnke, director and senior scientist at the Center for Fire, Rescue & EMS Health Research, NDRI-USA, Inc.

"Rothrock weaves together the elements of trauma and triumph. *After Trauma* is a valuable resource for those who live forward with the aftereffects of trauma, as well as for those of us who support and join with them on their journey by holding space both for them and with them."

—Lisa Zoll, LCSW, founder of Grief Relief

"Ali Rothrock rightly claims 'a loud voice that speaks hard truths.' Hers is a fierce, uncompromising voice for survivors, for surviving, for thriving. Listen to her voice and you will hear the echo of so many women and girls. Far too many. This book is a charge to men of conscience to find the courage to stand up. To speak up. To say, 'No more.' And a charge to women to believe in ourselves."

—jona olsson, fire and EMS chief, Latir Volunteer Fire Dept, Northern New Mexico, and founder of cultural bridges to justice

AFTER TRAUMA

AFTER TRAUMA

Lessons on
Overcoming
from a First
Responder
Turned Crisis
Counselor

ALI W. ROTHROCK

BROADLEAF BOOKS
MINNEAPOLIS

AFTER TRAUMA
Lessons on Overcoming from a First Responder Turned
Crisis Counselor

The author is represented by WordServeLiterary Group,
www.wordserveliterary.com.

Cover image: kyoshino/istock.com
Cover design: James Kegley

Print ISBN: 978-1-5064-8063-3
eBook ISBN: 978-1-5064-8064-0

To the healers, space holders,
and those who shine a light
in the darkness.

CONTENTS

CONTENTS

FOREWORD

Before I was shot on April 12, 2013, I hadn't experienced trauma. But that day, hiding in a closet inside the community college where I worked, with blood pouring out of my hand, I knew from that moment forward everything would be different. I understood even then that I was experiencing a clear delineation of time. There was before trauma, and now there would be after trauma.

In the aftermath of my recovery, I searched high and low for any resource I could find about trauma, grief, and healing. I bought any book I could find on the subject and stacked them up in a pile on the floor alongside my bed. The answers to my questions had to be in there. But as I poured over the books during the morning, the afternoon, and the middle of the night after a particularly horrible nightmare, I realized I wasn't actually looking for answers. I didn't even know what my questions were.

There is a theme that runs through a lot of books about trauma, be it memoirs or nonfiction, that if you approach your circumstances with a positive mindset and a determined spirit, everything will turn out okay—the ribbons of your story will be tied nicely into a bow once you reach the end. This is the theme I came across over and over again in my reading. I would read a story about someone who overcame something horrible and was living a great and fulfilling life, and instead of coming away inspired and encouraged, I felt even more angry and even more alone. *How nice for them*, I would think to myself, admittedly in a very sarcastic tone. Reading books written by or about people on the other side of their trauma wasn't helpful like I thought it would be. Because I wasn't on the other side of mine. It was impossible for me to see a world in which my days weren't marked by which doctor's appointment I needed to go to and how much pain medicine I needed to take. Imagining the rest of my life was a feat I suddenly couldn't accomplish when making it through the day was the best I could do.

It turns out that what I was looking for when I bought all those books, which I assume are all perfectly wonderful books, was just company in my grief. I simply wanted to read someone else's story and feel less alone. In the days following the shooting I was never alone, not physically anyway. There were always people around—loving me, supporting me, tending to my needs. But none of them had experienced what I had. None of them had a bullet wound in their body; and that separated us from one another. They couldn't know what I had been through. They couldn't feel what I was feeling no matter how hard they tried. So the stories from the other side just rang hollow. I wanted to read about trauma from someone sitting in it, someone who was willing to let it be without trying to cover it up or fix it. Someone who knew that it might not end nice and clean.

Turns out, this is hard to find. Mainly because people don't typically start writing their books about trauma from the very start. We write when we begin to process what happened, when we feel we have something to say about it, some wisdom to impart. Still, though, there are people who have the ability to write about their trauma from a strong and powerful place without feeling the need to pretend that you'll be able to go back to who you were before. That's what most of us want.

When I came across Ali's work a handful of years ago, I knew she was the real deal. I had that feeling in my bones reading her words about living through crises and experiencing horrific events, that I had found one of those people.

This book, *After Trauma*, is the book I needed to read back in 2013 during some of the darkest times of my life. Ali does something powerful in this book. In retelling her own personal story, she pulls up a chair next to us and makes sure we don't feel alone. In sharing her professional experiences as a first responder and her wisdom as a crisis counselor, she confidently assures us that she is the person to help guide us along our healing path, holding our stories gently in her hands.

Over the last nine years I have learned to be selective in who I let into my trauma, and the voices I allow to speak into my life and my healing. It's too tender and too important to let just anyone that close. It's too fragile to let just anyone have access to those parts of you. I wish now that I could have replaced that giant stack of books along the wall in my room with this one.

Since you've picked up this book, I am guessing you are in the midst of something difficult yourself, or maybe you are close to someone else who is, and you want to know how best to support them. Maybe you're feeling a little trepidation about opening yourself up to more words, more advice, more shoulds or to-dos. What you'll find within these pages is a friend, an advisor, a gentle yet empowering voice speaking into your life. No shame, criticism, or annoyingly pretty bows await you. You can trust this book you hold in your hands, and you can trust Ali as she walks with you through the pages.

—Taylor S. Schumann, author of *When Thoughts and Prayers Aren't Enough: A Shooting Survivor's Journey into the Realities of Gun Violence*

AUTHOR'S NOTE

Content warning:
This book contains descriptions of traumatic events,
including domestic violence and sexual assault.

This book reflects the author's present recollections of
experiences over time. Some names and characteristics
have been changed, some events have been compressed,
and some dialogue has been recreated.

INTRODUCTION

On May 22, 2017, a suicide bomber detonated a home-made explosive device just after an Ariana Grande concert in Manchester, England. When the news alert lit up my phone that night, I was sitting at my dining room table in Philadelphia, pen poised over a blank notebook page, eyes closed. Gabe Dixon's song "Disappear" played loudly in my headphones, a song from the album I play on an endless loop while writing. I'd been writing what would become this book for seven years by that point, but on that day, I'd felt I was on the verge of finding out what this book was truly supposed to be.

My newlywed husband turned on the news to see the preliminary reports of the terrorist attack. Cell phone footage of girls with cat-ear headbands running from the arena played on a loop as ambulances rushed toward the crowds. As girls continued to stream from the blast site, I watched them take their first steps as survivors away from immediate trauma and into their After. I wondered about who those girls would be a week after that day, a month, a year, about how that night would sit in their minds in some form forever. Who would they be when the concert stadium stopped smelling like firecrackers, when the last survivor left the hospital, when everyone else in their lives moved on? Who would they choose to be in the face of such a violent and unexpected disruption?

I thought of the choices I'd made about who I was going to be after trauma. Some choices I made consciously and took sustained effort; some I made in order to just survive and make it to the next day. What determined those choices? What would affect these brand-new survivors while making theirs? These questions hung in my brain like the smoke that still lingered among the arena seats in Manchester. That's when I knew I'd found the answer to what this book was meant to be.

After Trauma is not about focusing on suffering but on what comes next; it's about how ordinary people find the strength to keep going after all sorts of trauma. We've all heard about large-scale events like mass shootings or acts of terrorism. We are both fascinated and horrified by the fact that violence and tragedy can touch our lives at any time and in any number of ways. We learn the names of those lost and injured, and we might even follow their stories of recovery for a while.

But then that day fades, we forget the date it happened, and we move on. We are captivated by the next significantly tragic day and those lives lost and those injured . . . and so the cycle continues. We remember the number of those killed, maybe some bits and pieces of their lives, and the way they died. But we often forget that for those people who became famous in the worst way, their lives don't move on as quickly as ours do. Their overcoming is not complete when we forget about them. And what about the stories that never make the news, the stories we hold inside of us that aren't for public consumption? The moments of overcoming that are unknown and unwitnessed but just as significant? What about those whose job it is to respond to and witness moments of trauma?

As a little girl, I was carefree and cherished. I was taught that my ideas mattered and that the world would always work in favor of those who are striving for good. For the first sixteen years of my life, I trusted the adults around me and I trusted myself. But there was a moment many years ago when I sent that little girl away. She was too trusting, too innocent. She was too free. I sent her running out of a fire station while the rest of me stayed behind. I imagined her running through the parking lot, past the darkened churches, out of the crumbling graveyard, and up the hill toward home. I thought that when it was safe, I could just call her back to me. But the longer she stayed away, the more I felt the absence of what she took: my ability to trust and my ability to feel safe. That girl's homecoming was more than a decade in the making, and it happened without fanfare. It was only fitting that her homecoming would be surrounded by a fire truck's flashing lights. She came back to me after years of searching for her, after walking the cavernous valleys of my mind to bring her home.

For me and for most, the process of reconnecting to our lost selves was not linear, but it was cumulative. I had no rulebook or specific steps to follow to make sure I was "all better" in the end, but every step forward counted. I had to learn that I alone was responsible for the quality of my life, and I had to keep continuously choosing a path that propelled me toward the wholeness I sought. External changes contributed to finding this wholeness, but learning that I already had all that I needed to make a change is what got me there. I learned that dismissing the depths of pain didn't quicken this process but instead prolonged it. I eventually sought professional help because the trauma I'd experienced became the biggest part of me and was something I could no longer see around on my own. I needed company while doing the work necessary to move forward with the rest of my life. This journey was fueled by a simple desire to know who I could be if I could find a way to climb out of the mental valley I'd become stuck in. I wanted to know what the view from the summit would look like. This process was also fueled by a desire to regain my autonomy and voice and the hope that putting in that work would carve out a path others could follow.

I learned that trauma separates by design. It leaves us divided into our before and after—a split that demands to be noticed. Our hurt demands to be acknowledged. I also learned that the place of trauma, the literal or figurative place of that disconnection, can be the place where we come back to our past selves and reemerge. It can be the new foundation we stand on. A reconciliation. A rebirth. We can come home to ourselves and find our *Afters*. I did, eventually.

This book came in intentional spurts, a purposeful unfolding of an entire decade of growth and reclaiming what had been taken from me. Some seasons are for overcoming and some seasons are for becoming the person who will overcome. This book details both.

This book is for you, a survivor, especially those of you whose experiences do not fit the expected or accepted narrative of survivorship. This book is for you who are carrying dreams, for you who have had to fight against broken systems, and for you who have had to endlessly rally and rise to keep your fire lit. It's for you who have struggled with your mental health as a result of trauma from on-the-job first responder experiences, at-home experiences, childhood adversity, a onetime trauma, cumulative trauma, genetics, or a combination of these factors. This book is for you who are raging against societal expectations and for you who are in all stages of overcoming a variety of life's injuries. For you who are trying every day to reclaim and redefine your life. And this book is for you who are trying to understand how to help a loved one who is struggling.

My dad had a subarachnoid brain hemorrhage in 2008 that left him semicomatose in the neurological ICU for twelve days. As my family grappled with the visceral panic of potentially losing him, he was knocked out on morphine in a helicopter, having no awareness of the indescribable fear we were experiencing. Miraculously, he recovered with no deficits or long-term impacts. Recently, I asked him about his After.

"It was a reset," he told me. "You don't need trauma to grow or make changes. But if you are recovering from a difficult experience, you do have a choice, even if you didn't choose what happened to you. You can decide to grow."

That concept became the point of this story: not to focus on my or others' trauma but to hold space for those examples of overcoming and resilience. In the following pages, I've collected some of those stories in addition to telling mine. Thank you for bearing witness to us.

PART I

And when you go through the valley
And the shadow comes down from the hill
If morning never comes to be
Be still, be still, be still

If you forget the way to go
And lose where you came from
If no one is standing beside you
Be still and know I am

—The Fray

1

FORGIVE YOURSELF
FOR NOT SEEING IT COMING

Compromise where you can. Where you can't, don't.
Even if everyone is telling you that something wrong
is something right. Even if the whole world is telling
you to move, it is your duty to plant yourself like a tree,
look them in the eye, and say "No, you move."
                                        —Christopher Markus

I've been able to recite my story with crystal-clear accuracy for over a decade now. I could always deliver the entire thing chronologically, with the events laid out like a sterile and tidy timeline of trauma. I thought that was my mark of overcoming—that being able to tell the story with no emotion meant I was carrying no burden. But the narrative I'd been telling was only half realized. The black-and-white timeline was just the backdrop, the bones. A question mark hovered over the events, casting a shadow that hung itself over my shoulders and crawled inside my mind like a parasite.

I had internalized a quiet blame, an attempt to find order in the chaos that had come from a long-lasting violation. I clung desperately to an old belief that impending trauma was always preceded by omens or warning signs that would signal one to change course to avoid the impending catastrophe and that I'd simply missed mine.

I felt anger at myself for being careless, and this made me feel complicit in the choices others made to hurt me. It took time and intention for me to see that the shadow of blame never belonged on my shoulders. I didn't miss any prophecy. Not having a crystal ball to see the danger ahead didn't make me an accomplice. This realization shone a light on the shadow and made it dissipate like smoke. Occasionally, when I'm speaking in front of a crowd these days, I talk about this realization and my voice starts coming out of me in waves. The appropriate emotion is present now, and it feels like the empowering antithesis of the shadow I shed. I shed the shadow by going back to the beginning, by going back to the place where I'd lost her, my younger self.

It was the summer of 2014. I remember it being cool for late July. I walked through my grandparents' house, looking at the toys my cousins and I had played with during our past summers there. I stopped in the doorway and suddenly felt a sense of all the time that had passed since I considered myself a child. Some of us grow up gradually, arriving at adulthood slowly and through a culmination of our experiences up to that point. My growing up occurred suddenly, almost violently, like a sudden, soaking thunderstorm.

When my sibling Julia and I were younger, I felt an overwhelming sense of responsibility. While at the roller skating rink for a birthday party, I would crane my neck to keep Julia in view.

"There are adults there," my mom would tell me beforehand. "You can just have fun. It's the adults' job to look after you both."

I still believed her words when I walked into the fire service. My privileged sense of security had never been challenged. I willingly stepped into my new world at this first firehouse, having no concept that danger was staring right back at me. My thirty-two-year-old self can see that what was coming was clear from the very beginning. My sixteen-year-old self thought that their smiles meant I was welcome there. I had no idea smiles could mean something else entirely.

As a girl, I was often asked, "Ali, what do you want to do when you grow up? Who do you want to be?" and I would get worried, as if I was going to go to sleep one night and awake the next day as a different person of my choosing. My mom says I was often concerned because I didn't know how I was ever going to make that choice.

I wanted to be a hairdresser, then a singer, a teacher, a veterinarian, a marine biologist, and an Olympic ice skater. Then after ice skating, I became obsessed with the movie *Twister* and wanted to be a tornado chaser with my best friend Matt. But then I found firefighting, and every single thing in my life aligned. Firefighting was my missing piece. I felt like we'd always been looking for each other.

My great-grandfather, Carl James Peterson, was the fire chief of Stanford Hose Company in Corry, Pennsylvania. During a fire in the late sixties, he found the body of a little girl who'd been suffocated as she hid in a closet. He carried her body out of the fire and, as my Uncle Terry wrote in his biography, "the emotion of that incident stayed with him forever." Then on Easter Sunday, 1970, five Stanford Hose Company firefighters were killed at the Sherwin-Williams paint store when it exploded during a fire. Great-grandpa CJP was burned on his hands, arms, and face as he worked to save those firefighters. I always thought that my desire to be a firefighter came out of the clear, blue sky, but when I learned about my great-grandfather, I felt so proud that I was carrying on this tradition. His love for firefighting skipped two generations until I found it again.

I grew up in the fire service. I don't mean literally. I haven't been around fire trucks my whole life, and I'm not a legacy firefighter unless you count my great-grandfather, which no one ever does. I grew up in the fire service in the sense that once I joined the fire service, I grew up.

On an October day in 2005, I walked into that first firehouse as a sixteen-year-old and felt like I finally had an answer to both of the questions posed to me as a child. Firefighting was what I wanted to do, and a firefighter was who I wanted to be. It was National Fire Prevention Week—a time when most firehouses have an open house. At this station, they'd set up a mock house fire, complete with a burning hay bale, and were offering members of the community the opportunity to put on fire gear and put it out.

To the surprise of my entire family, I eagerly stood in that line and waited my turn. To this day, I can't tell you what made me do it. I put on gear that was way too big and followed a firefighter with a white helmet (I would learn that this signified he was a chief) as we crawled forward with a hose line in our hands to put out the fire on the small bale of hay. In disbelief, Julia snapped some pictures as I was waiting to put out the fire, and when I look back on them now, I see a look on my face that I don't think I'd ever seen before. It was determination, focus, drive. Putting on that fire gear, even though it was two sizes too big, made me feel at home.

As soon as I'd taken the gear off, I eagerly wanted to do more. The chief smiled and told me that they were running out of hay and that I couldn't have another turn, but did I want an application to join their fire company?

I've asked myself many times in the years since, Why did he offer that to me? Did he expect that I would fall in line with what would end up being expected of me? Did he want me around for entertainment? Did any part of him see the passion I had for firefighting as something he wanted to nurture or was it always just a joke? As I filled out the application and handed it back in to the appointed firefighter, I remember the look on that man's face. It seemed as though I had made him really angry, but I couldn't figure out why. Looking back, I now see this as my first indication of what was coming, the first trickle of blood on a wound that had been festering for generations.

I came home, found a half-full journal, and jotted down a few lines about what I had done and who I had met. That became a habit. Every day I came home and wrote down what I was learning. I thought it would be important to be able to look back at those beginning days and remember what falling in love had been like. I wanted to always be able to relish that feeling, and I wanted to remember every single thing I learned there. I felt so incredibly lucky that I had found my purpose at the age of sixteen.

In those first few months, I learned so much. I learned how to pull 150 feet of folded hose line off the side of a fire engine and place it on my shoulder. I learned how to lift ladders up and "throw them" against the side of the firehouse. I learned how to run up to a fire hydrant, wrap it with the dry five-inch hose, remove the cap with the clunky hydrant wrench, flush it until the water ran clean, hook up the hose, and charge the line. I learned how to get dressed in my gear as fast as possible and cover up every speck of skin to protect it against flames. I learned how to train my ears to make out every single word of the sometimes garbled dispatcher voices as they alerted the firefighters to an emergency. I bought fire-fighting shirts, books, and a silver Maltese cross necklace that became my most prized possession.

But I also learned to resent my body and view it in a way I never had before. This new environment told me it was too feminine, that it gave me away, that it had no place in this masculine world. I hated how I couldn't hide my body because some men saw it and wanted to own it, to dominate it because it was way too much and yet nowhere near enough.

A few weeks after I started, I sat on the floor of the engine bay one night with an air pack (what firefighters wear on their backs to bring breathable air into fires where the superheated gases could sear your lungs immediately) on the ground in front of me. I had my fire gloves on, which fit me like giant oven mitts. They did not have gloves that fit me and hadn't bothered to order any, so I got the same size every other guy was given. I was practicing changing the air cylinder on the back of the air pack, as I knew that, in the event of a fire, replacing people's spent air cylinders with fresh ones was an easy skill I could perform before I received much other training. Removing the cylinder required dexterity, which I did not have while wearing those oven mitts, but I knew that if that air pack was in a heated environment, the metal could be hot, so the gloves needed to stay on. So I sat on the floor and practiced. *Cylinder in. Step 1, 2, 3, it's ready for use. Step 3, 2, 1, cylinder is out and ready to change.*

It was quiet. Peaceful. Almost reverent. I was always hoping for a call, ready to move at the slightest squawk from the small black pager I clipped to the back pocket of my jeans. And then a nameless firefighter walked by, paying no attention to me. I called after him, asking a question about some fire call scenario I'd made up in my mind. I wanted to know exactly what the protocol was, what role I should play on the scene if this made-up emergency happened. He turned back to face me but paused long enough for me to think he didn't hear me. I was about to ask my question in another way when he responded and forever changed the way I saw the world and my place in it.

He shone the first light on my cage—a cage of expectation that existed just for me, a girl. This nameless firefighter finally spoke: "I hear your question and I will answer your question . . . but first I want you to go into that closet where [guy's name] is waiting and let the light stay off. Let whatever happens happen and don't tell anyone. And then I will answer your question."

Back then, I didn't have all the words I have now. But I knew that it was a disgusting suggestion and was simply something I wanted no part of. I put the air pack away, walked out of the station, and drove home, my world tilting slightly off its axis.

When I tell this part of the story in front of a crowd, I always pause right here. I want to see people's faces as they process this in real time. I want them to think about what this means, about what our world can ask of women and girls and of what he was asking of me. They shake their heads slightly, they wrinkle their noses. The men look at me with pity; the women look at me with a *knowing*.

Another time, I was told someone was "waiting for me" in his car, in the part of the parking lot where the cone of light from the streetlight didn't reach. I was invited to go "talk" to him. All of this was asked of me so they could make it "easier for me there." They said it with mischievous laughter in their eyes, telling me that it was my way to freedom when really it would have just solidified my bondage.

It was an offer for an exchange in a context they understood. My compliance, my silence, and unprotested access to my body were the currency. *Follow our rules*, they told me. *Laugh when we make a rape joke. Smile when we talk about how your "young boobs" would look during a wet T-shirt contest. Continue to make eye contact when we speak graphically about the mechanics of sex and when we play porn on the TV in the lounge. Don't look away. Don't ever look away. Make dirty jokes back at us so we know you aren't a prude. But stay pure enough so we can say, "Ali isn't like those other girls."*

This was my payment for acceptance into their world. Only then would my existence be allowed. I am forever grateful, truly and deeply grateful, that I knew this treatment was wrong. All my life, I'd grown up with the antidote to it. My mom and dad were true partners in every sense of the word. Life wasn't split into roles based on gender in my house. Julia and I were taught how to use a socket wrench just as much as we were taught how to use a garden trowel. I'd seen the way my parents treated each other with love and respect and was taught that I deserved that in all my relationships too, so when this started, I was able to fight so hard against it because I knew it didn't have to be this way.

An older firefighter sent me thirty-five text messages in two days, saying things like "I just need to remind myself how old you are" and telling me that he was sitting outside of my house in the middle of the night. In passing once, someone told me that they knew which window in my house was my bedroom. I wasn't sure exactly how to interpret that. Were they going to come crawling through it one night as I slept in the same room as Julia? None of this felt like it was up for debate. It just was. I was trying to rapidly understand this truth. It was a life-altering and irrevocable truth that I could never unlearn or unsee. Once I saw it, once I truly understood the reality of this situation, I could never again close my eyes to the cage I was being asked to live in. As soon as I stepped out of the cage—a cage where I was confined by their expectations—I was no longer the sum of myself. I was seen as an antagonizer. A brazen outlier. The reasons I joined the fire service didn't matter. I was no longer *me* to them. They didn't want who I was. They wanted someone who would coyly roll their eyes but not open their mouth. Refusing the cage meant that, in their eyes, I was entitled, spoiled, prudish, a tease. "Go ahead and call the cops," I was told. "That'll just make it worse for you."

I never bartered. I never traded myself for better treatment or an easier passage, because that too was a lie. Nothing was ever going to be easy for me there. My looks had never been so complimented. But even back then, I saw the explicit flattery for the trap that it was. It was all so thinly veiled even to my sixteen-year-old self. I wrote in my journal after just a few months there, "They told me I was beautiful in a way that knows no freedom."

I displayed defiance by simply existing there. Just showing up for calls or to training or to vote at a company meeting was seen as "disobedient" within their narrow definition of female obedience. I never wished I was different, never wished I could just be happy in my cage. *No,* I thought, *these men are wrong. This world is wrong. Their expectations are wrong. This cage is wrong. I am not wrong.*

"I was just kidding."

"She can't take a joke."

"She's so sensitive."

These comments were usually made as the harasser was smiling as if they were telling a joke I just didn't understand. And that was always their excuse, anyway. I was being aggressively gaslit before I knew the term. I didn't have words to describe what was going on there, and explaining it to anyone but the pages of my journal felt humiliating: "They talk about what they want to do to me..."

After all, firefighting was what I felt put on this earth to do. Coming to the terms with the environment I had to do it in felt like just another thing I needed to learn. For all I knew, this is what firefighting was like everywhere. Years later after this trauma had ended, I would stand on a very public stage and say, "Being a part of that fire house felt like a zero sum game, like I had to make a decision. I could give it all up and be rid of the environment that was hurting me or I could put up with it all and keep doing this thing that I loved. I felt like I had no good options."

After just a month there, my inaugural fire call came. It was the first ahead of hundreds of others, but it was easily the most significant. It showed me the power, beauty, and significance of emergency services. It takes some firefighters years to arrive at a call like this one, but for me, I got it right out of the gate. I think back to that night often, but not for the reasons people might think. I can still see the little girl there, her black skin standing out against the white sheets of the ambulance's litter. I can see the coating of snow on the road, the blood on her face, and the little pink butterfly clips on the ends of her braids. As tragic as this was, it wasn't the death that replays in my mind. What stood out at the time and what would propel me to making a big decision thirteen years later was the lack of care those firefighters gave to themselves when we got back to the station.

No peer supporters (first responders trained to recognize if a fellow first responder is struggling and connect them to resources) were brought in, nor was a CISM (critical incident stress management) team made up of first responders and mental health specialists trained to respond to and support first responders after a traumatic incident. We had nothing.

That night, the engine bay was silent but filled with firefighters who must have been reliving the call in their minds. No one said a word. Even though these men would torture me in many ways, I kept coming back to the lack of care that was given to them after that incident. What could have helped lessen the impact of this traumatic event for all of us? I wondered how many times that had happened. How many traumas had they seen and been a part of that had gone unacknowledged?

By the time I got back home, the rest of my family was asleep. I stood in our darkened living room and stared out the front window at the snow that was still falling. Since there had been no conversation at the station, I had to find resolve alone. I took stock of myself and laid out what I knew as clearly as I could see it at the time.

I had just witnessed the aftermath of the violent death of a child. I knew that this was pretty much as bad a situation as I could be a part of as a first responder. While on the scene, I hadn't had the urge to cry, throw up, or turn away. I hadn't felt like I was going to lose my composure at any point. Instead, I wanted to know what decisions were made in terms of getting her out of the car as fast as possible. I wanted to have been in the ambulance where the firefighters assisted the paramedics as they tried to bring life back into her body. I didn't want to run away from her. I wanted to run toward her. I also knew that in a similar situation in the future, we might actually be able to save the victim. That filled me with so much motivation I almost wanted to return to the station right then and teach myself something that might have helped her. And so, standing in my childhood living room, while I was being told all of these "truths" from abusive men, sixteen-year-old Ali decided an irrevocable truth of her own.

I decided that the sense of being at home that I had felt when I put on fire gear for the first time wasn't wrong. I decided that I belonged in this world because I had stayed in the game that night—mentally and emotionally—which, as it turns out, is the majority of the work on emergency scenes. I had stayed in the game in a world that so far had only wanted me if I participated from inside the cage. I'd refused those expectations and knew I could stay true to myself. I knew that if I could just survive this place, I could find a firehouse where I was safe and accepted. I just proved to myself that my mind and stomach were strong. I could train my muscles to do the rest. I'd been a firefighter for just over one month, but already I knew that I was going to be involved with the fire service for the rest of my life.

That decision, that belief, that *knowing* would carry me through my future walk through the valley. I would lose parts of myself in their hatred for me. But nothing would ever shake the decision I made on that night. I welded the door of the cage shut, knowing that for the rest of my life, I would never forget what was asked of me in that firehouse, nor would I be quiet about it. I would never forget the unwavering belief that I had then and still have now that I could succeed exactly as I was without changing, removing, or adding parts of myself.

The incident that night would remain both a violent and a hopeful reminder. It reminded me of the worst kind of death but also of the people who weren't afraid to look it in the face, to say, "Not now, not here." Those firefighters did everything that they could to save her, and to me, that is purely good. Every push on her chest, every breath from their lungs into hers, was an exchange, a sacrifice, an act of love. It showed me that people are not entirely bad or entirely good, but that they can hold a conflicting amount of both. And there were so many times when I wanted to categorize my fellow firefighters as only bad, but that would be an incorrect simplification. No one is simply one or the other but a sum of their choices.

My dissension and my refusal to follow the rules made these men furious, but it made the chase that much more fervent. "Getting" me was their goal. Corrupting me was their focus. Learning how to be a great firefighter was mine, at first. But then learning how to survive them and remain *me* became all I could focus on.

After just a few months there, still believing in the leadership and the idea of consequences, I submitted a formal complaint of sexual harassment to the fire company's disciplinary committee. As a result, one person was suspended for thirty days. Removing one of the loudest offenders might have seemed like a fix, but it was like placing a Band-Aid on a gangrenous wound.

In early middle school, my parents realized that I needed glasses. I remember the world-changing perspective shift those wire frames allowed me. We drove home after that eye appointment, and I kept exclaiming at all the detail I could now see: the leaves on the trees, the cracks in the sidewalks, the writing on billboards. These experiences in my first firehouse were like that first pair of glasses—perspective-shifting and eye-opening. They showed me what was always there that I'd never noticed before.

One hot summer evening, we were doing search and rescue training in the acquired structure a few streets down from my house. The purpose was to completely black out our environment, then teach the firefighters to move through the rooms as if we were searching for victims during a fire, maintaining communication with our partner, and going up and down the stairs safely. We staple-gunned black plastic over the windows and plugged in the smoke machine. Dressed in my gear and breathing through an air pack, I got to my knees and prepared to begin as they shut the door, my right hand resting on my partner's boot in front of me. The objective was to get comfortable in the dark. I remember being surprised by the completeness of the blackness, the totality of it. It was disorienting to know that my eyes were open, but I couldn't make out anything in my surroundings. I realized that if I closed my eyes, the darkness was something I could control, and therefore, I no longer felt overcome by it. I then felt comfortable finding my way.

The firefighters assured me that I would be claustrophobic and would not be able to complete the training, but I did so with a happy exhilaration that would accompany me on trainings for the next fifteen years.

Whenever things started to get really bad in that fire-house, I looked for ways to be able to control that darkness too. I didn't yet know about coping skills. I didn't know that our brains are excellent at adapting to pain but that sometimes the ways we find to cope help us in the moment but become maladaptive habits that end up hurting us in the long term.

The summer after I graduated high school, a kind fellow firefighter invited me on a ride-along to a department in a different state to hopefully get a better experience. He knew how desperately I needed it and was doing what he could to show me that the firehouse environment could be different. On the way, I made a deal with myself, with God, and with the universe. I told myself if I could just meet one nice firefighter, just one person who treated me like I was a human being aside from my body parts, then I would know that my belief in goodness was not misplaced, that I could find a good firehouse somewhere, that good firefighters did exist. I just had to stay in the game long enough to find it.

We traveled a few hours south in the middle of summer. It was stiflingly hot, but I wore my standard chosen uniform during that time: oversized, dark blue sweat-pants and a sweatshirt. For years by that point, I refused to show even a bit of skin from my neck to my toes. I was so used to feeling overexposed, violated by eyes and comments. I'd stopped wearing much makeup and cut my hair short. I had learned to hide in subtle ways, to reduce or eliminate parts of my femininity as a way to try to shrink the target on my back.

We responded to many calls that day, including standing below a bridge while a woman up above threatened to jump and to throw over the baby in her arms too. We landed a helicopter for a little boy who had been hit by a beer truck. He was barely alive; his little broken body lay in the grass on someone's front lawn as the neighborhood gathered around. When the helicopter landed, the wind from it blew my shirt up, exposing me up to my white sports bra. I turned around to see a row of sunglasses-wearing firefighters grinning maliciously. I felt violated by the eyes on my bare skin. I realized then that this firehouse was no different from mine. All day it had been the same comments, the same unsettling feeling of lurking danger. Earlier in the day, they'd pressed play on the TV as I walked into the lounge and hardcore porn began to play loudly. They compared me to the naked and moaning girls on the screen.

I felt like I was slipping farther away from myself from being in these environments. I'd had to send parts of me too far away in an attempt to protect them. I was always on high alert for danger. I was careful not to be alone in a room with anyone. These things felt normal and necessary to me at the time, but looking back, I see how unfair it all was.

We returned to the station after responding to a serious car accident. A man had rolled a box truck onto its side at a high speed, and either in the accident or as he made his way out of the shattered driver's-side window, he severed the main artery that ran up the side of his neck. As we got there, a passerby was kneeling over him, putting pressure onto his wound and trying to keep him alive long enough for help to arrive. When she removed her hand to let a firefighter take over, the man had a seizure. His blood sprayed out onto the pavement like a gory garden hose, and the flashing lights of the fire trucks began to reflect in it. A helicopter quickly arrived, landing in the shut-down roadway not far from the accident scene. At the hospital, I knew that man would have all the help available to hopefully save his life.

As I sat at the kitchen table after this call, I was ping-ponging back and forth between the disgusting dichotomy I'd found in the fire service. I didn't want to walk away from this job, but the more I experienced it, the less I wanted to spend time in fire stations. Every firefighter I'd met in the previous three years was someone who was willing to put themselves in harm's way to help complete strangers. Every firefighter I'd met was willing to leave their family to respond to an emergency, willing to stand outside in the blistering heat or a blustery blizzard to be a part of helping someone else. But there was another side to many of them. There was a switch they flipped when behind closed doors—a switch that meant I wasn't safe. I knew I was tired, deep in my soul. I knew that three years of dealing with this dichotomy was depleting me. Sitting at that firehouse kitchen table in the wee hours of the morning, I was alone. Some firefighters milled around in the kitchen, making coffee to start their day. Some went back to bed. No one spoke to me. I was determined to find some vestige of goodness to hang onto in the job. I felt like it was slipping through my fingers. But I thought of the little girl from my first car accident and the man who we'd just loaded into a helicopter. I knew that if I got up and went to bed to sleep through the next few hours until the ride-along was over, I would wake up exhausted enough to walk away, simply too depleted to continue fighting against the cage. But in that moment at that kitchen table, I felt defiant and stubborn. I decided that I wasn't going to get up and go to bed. I was going to sit at that table and wait until one single person interacted with me in a way that was positive, or at least not negative.

A few minutes after settling on this thought, I heard the door bang open to my left. Three firefighters stumbled in, and I immediately realized that they were not sober. I didn't even want to turn my head to look at them as I felt the need to draw as little attention to myself as possible. Every thought of how to stay in the fire service left my mind, and for the first but not last time in my life, alarm bells started going off in my mind. My gut told me to make myself safe, and my mind flashed to the lock on the women's bathroom, which felt impossibly far away on the other side of the building. I moved next door into the darkened lounge and hid. When they walked into that room, my self-preservation instincts told me to hold my breath to be as quiet as possible. Somehow, I don't know how, I was discovered in the dark.

I wonder now, Did they plan what happened? Would they have found me wherever I was in the firehouse when they returned home? Had I inadvertently made it easier for them due to my location in the building when they arrived? Or was it a crime of convenience? Did they do it because they could? Did one of them choose it and the others simply followed? Did they take that action because they thought, as many people who sexually assault others do, that they wouldn't be held accountable because they could just blame how drunk they were? As if that means they are innocent.

Rape culture is an escalating spectrum, with seemingly "harmless" microaggressive actions like rape jokes on one end and physical rape on the other. So much of the spectrum had been allowed and actively encouraged in that station. I'd been seeing the all-too-familiar signs since I arrived, but I didn't know how much danger it put me in.

Rape culture can also be thought of as a pyramid. Every time someone expresses a sexist attitude and it is met with silence by those who hear it, *the act and the response to it* lay the foundation for the next step in potentially intensifying behavior. Witnesses who do nothing aren't innocent. Their silence isn't harmless. That's the glue that holds the whole thing together. In any environment, if the objectification of women is seen as normal and even incentivized, if the boundary-crossing has become standard practice, since the degradation of our entire gender has been baked into the very core of our culture, a physical violation is simply a natural evolution. It aggravates me when people act surprised that sexual assaults are so prevalent and when they feign shock when the latest rapist is defended by the statement that being legally held accountable for committing the witnessed rape of an unconscious person is "a steep price to pay for twenty minutes of action." Our society perpetuates this pyramid in active and passive ways because it works for the gender in most positions of power and helps keep them there.

Writer Nina Alter tells us that sexism, like all the other "isms," is a problem of culture, and this culture is perpetuated by the choices individuals make based on the roles we've all been taught men and women "should" take in our society. And by "we all," I mean our ancestors and our ancestors' ancestors. This didn't start with us; we've just picked up the torch and kept it lit. Sexism is not solitary disparate incidents like rape, catcalling, or someone refusing to work with or for a woman based on her gender. These actions are not separate from each other but rather pieces of the same huge, dysfunctional puzzle that our society continues to hold together.

In work environments, the people who have been around a while perpetuate the culture, the leadership allows it, and the newer people quickly get indoctrinated. Then they maintain it through their own comments and actions. And so the cycle goes. And then in my case, a firehouse gets a female firefighter, and she says, "Hang on, this environment sucks," but it's easier to blame her and call her uptight than to actually look at the problem that exists and what sort of actions will have to be taken to stop the cycle we are all caught in. The culture of this firehouse had already normalized treating women as sexual objects, degrading us as less than human. All it took was one more choice to take it all the way.

Since the attack happened in an interior room with the lights off, I couldn't see anything, and so my memories of that night come from my other senses. My memories are of our limbs tangling, three against one, and me trying to find myself underneath them. I remember a rough and sweaty sandpaper-like hand curling around my throat, fingers squeezing, dominating, silencing, owning. I remember a hand on the skin of my stomach underneath my shirt, fingers brushing against the waistband of my sweatpants.

I was so beaten down. I was so used to what was happening to me not even causing a blip on the radar of others. That night, there was a brief resignation, a fleeting thought of *Just get it over with*. That thought hammered into my brain as I heard my rapidly rising heartbeat in my ears. My heartbeat reminded me that I was still alive, still breathing. I didn't know the physical violation would be there, in that strange firehouse, on that dirty couch, but I knew it would be somewhere. It had long been insinuated that if I didn't willingly give "it," eventually, someone was going to try to take it. Refusal and choice collided. And when it came, when it was literally upon me, I just wanted it over with. I wanted it over with so I could leave the fire service with a flip of my middle finger and never, ever return. I wanted to light the cage of expectation on fire and burn it all down.

At a time when I thought it couldn't get any worse, when the trauma had been accumulating on top of itself, when my instinct was to push the pain away or stay busy enough not to notice it, this event shocked my body enough to freeze me in place. Immobilized with fear, I didn't know if fighting would make it worse, more violent. It was a horrendous choice.

While I was frozen underneath them, I had a brief image of myself walking out of that firehouse after they had finished with me, and in that image, I saw a shadow of my full self, like I would leave a part of me behind right there where I lay if what was about to happen happened.

That thought scared me enough to move, to fight, to think, *Fuck you and fuck this*, NO, and I felt my body charge with visceral electricity. It was three years of potential energy. After the sustained harassment from my fellow firefighters, after the everyday dichotomy, the betrayals, the cage, this energy had been building up in my blood. And when it was finally released, I had enough strength to get them off me and get myself away from them. I remember throwing my elbow and feeling it connect with something solid, maybe someone's chest. One fell, then the other moved enough for me to move, then the last one, and I was free. I know how fortunate I am that there were no weapons involved. I know that fighting back often worsens the violence of sexual assault and can even lead to murder, but in my case, fighting saved me. I know that their inebriation was a factor that helped me because when I pushed them off me, they fell to the ground instead of fighting back.

My body would hold the memory of that night for more than a decade. For the longest time, I could only remember them walking into the lounge, backlit by the light of the kitchen, and then me running out of that room in the other direction. I did not have the memory of whatever happened in between. My brain thought it was doing me a kindness by not remembering, and I was honestly OK with that memory gap for a while. But years later, when I started trying to reassemble myself, I wanted to remember everything, even if the worst possible thing happened in there.

My first book, *Where Hope Lives*, discusses what happened that night briefly, but it's easy to miss what actually happened because I could only use the words I had at the time. It wasn't until I started to heal from other experiences that I was able to realize the gravity of the event. We don't always need to go back to the beginning or dig into an event to heal from it, but I needed to shovel out the shame and sadness I'd piled on top of every event, especially this one, to get to the root of it, the hurt of it. Only then could I allow my younger self to feel the grief she'd deserved to feel at the time.

The versions of ourselves that got hurt are still in us, no matter how much time has passed. The sadness is still there, no matter how much we pile on top of it to keep the feeling at bay, no matter how practiced we are at ignoring it, at denying the pain what it needs: to be heard.

In the days after the assault, I didn't say much to anyone. I alluded to it with some people, but I had been so conditioned to expect disbelief and blame for my own abuse that I thought I was protecting myself from that eventuality by just staying silent. I thought that because I didn't see this coming, I was somehow responsible.

Family friends and former elementary school teachers would say, "Ali, you're a firefighter? That's so cool! What's it like?" I would think of Julia. I would think of my parents. They didn't deserve any of the ugliness that I felt could descend upon them as a result of me speaking the full truth. And so I lied, softening the edges of my reality. I would smile and talk about how exciting the fire calls are and how tough but fun the training is, and I stopped there. And then lying became a habit. I pushed the truth so far down that, after a while, it became harder and harder to access. In spite of it all, I stood up against their beliefs, their expectations, their cage. It was horrifyingly lonely, but it didn't feel like a conscious choice I made as much as instinct. After walking into this environment and realizing the reality of it, I immediately went to war.

My parents still ask themselves how they didn't know. I didn't tell them the worst of it because I knew they would make me leave firefighting, and I was too stubborn. I wasn't telling them in an effort to protect them, which was not my job. And they didn't know how much my mental health was suffering and how I was going to be impacted long term, because I didn't know. All of this was happening to me, but I was barely comprehending the significance of it. That's what happens with trauma. Often, some far away part of our brains knows that something bad, something worse than anything we've felt before, is happening. But we don't yet have the language or perspective to know exactly what and exactly how it will manifest in us. In that firehouse, each bit of harassment felt like another punch to a bruise that never had enough time to heal before the next punch came. Each bit of cumulative trauma was a drop in a bucket that I kept from overflowing for a long time out of sheer willpower, but one day, I just wasn't able to anymore.

Imagine holding a five-pound weight in your hand with your arm parallel to the ground. You can hold it steady for a while, but eventually, your arm will start to shake under the weight of it. Someone would see that and think, *Why are they struggling with such a small weight? It wouldn't be too heavy for me!* But what they don't know is how long you've been holding it. They don't know that you've never put the weight down, that you've never allowed anyone else to help you hold it. And then an experience adds another five-pound weight and another and another, and eventually, you just can't hold it up anymore. That's cumulative stress. We can hold many experiences for a while, but without rest and support, we will eventually drop the weight and our well-being will suffer.

There were some bright spots. There was a firefighter who helped me study for upcoming tests, told me about significant calls he'd run to help me think through strategy and tactics, and tried to shield me from some of the worst of it. Another, a dispatcher by trade, arranged for me to shadow a few different dispatchers to get to see another side of the emergency services and get me out of that firehouse. Another firefighter, an instructor, arranged for me to be able to take the 180-hour entry-level firefighting course specifically at our station and ensured that my eighteenth birthday would coincide with the final module, a structure burn, so I could fully participate and certify as an adult. You have to be eighteen years old to complete the final module. Each of these bright spots of normalcy and acceptance allowed me time to catch my breath, as this was truly what I knew the fire service could be. But because the system we were operating in was never set up to give me, a woman, equal opportunities, because this station tried to make me fit into the outdated mold that already existed instead of realizing that we all needed a different mold that could fit more than just one type of person, those bright spots didn't add up to a substantial change in the culture or environment.

I'd heard some of the firefighters had held a meeting where they discussed my faults and critiqued my body. Around that same time, there was a building fire where the cylinder on my air pack had been purposefully emptied, and I'd been sent into a fire with no air to breathe. When I rushed out of the building seeking air that wouldn't burn my lungs, having realized whose hands had last touched my air pack, the firefighters standing there used this as "proof that I couldn't hang." A reoccurring dream of suffocating began that night. Who'd done it was an open secret, and as an attempt at a consequence, the leadership put together a "task force" to monitor the air in the cylinders. The firefighter who had emptied my cylinder was put in charge of this task force. I remember the man who told me that, laughing as he said it. My entire existence felt like a joke.

My third winter in the firehouse, they took an egregious and desperately selfish step to rid themselves of me completely. I don't know whose idea it was, who gave it validity, how many others justified it, or how many knew of it, but a petition was put together and signed by an unknown number of firefighters, people who had presumably joined the fire company to help members of their community when they needed it. Everyone who signed the petition pledged to not respond to calls if I was there. Even as used to this bullshit as I was, I did not believe it at first. No one could be that selfish. No one could hate me so much that they would not respond to someone's call for help. But sure enough, for an entire month, any time I was there for a call, people would walk into the station, see me getting my gear on or sitting in the back of the engine, and walk right back out.

I'd finally had enough. I attempted to get justice from the profession I believed could give it to me. I sat in the front of a patrol car claiming that I wanted to do a ride-along because I was considering becoming a police officer. I thought that if anyone saw me and questioned it, I could tell the lie convincingly to avoid further retaliation. As we drove, I told the police officer what was happening in the station, what had been going on for years—the harassment, the threats, the hate, the empty cylinder. Forcing myself to be brave, I pulled a piece of paper from my pocket on which I'd scribbled down every person's name I'd been told had signed the petition. I waited on a knife's edge for his response, wholly desperate to be seen.

"Boys will be boys, won't they?" the officer finally said without looking at me, lazily turning the steering wheel. I waited for him to correct himself, to say he misspoke, to be on my side. But as he went on to mention some bullshit about "human nature," I just stopped listening, unable to bear the disappointment. An almost universal feeling for survivors of sexual or gender-based trauma is the fear of not being believed, and it's not hard to see why: because that's so often what we are met with. It's easier to hate the truth-tellers instead of the truth, and we can turn that hate onto ourselves.

That night, searching for answers, I told myself that I must not have used the right words or hadn't given him enough examples to make him understand. I put the blame for that man choosing to participate in the system of sexism on my shoulders along with everything else. It had taken me so much mental preparation to sit in that patrol car, so much faith that just *for once* I would be seen by someone who had power over the situation, but that man failed me because he chose to take the easy way forward from the conversation, leaving me alone.

I think of the version of me who was sitting in that police car. She was in so much pain. She was trying so hard to keep it together for everyone else. I wish she could have known what I know now. I wish she could have known that one day, more police officers than her memory can hold would apologize for this officer's failure; that one day, the profession that tried to erase her would respond with so much love, it would be staggering; that she would take that feeling of being thrown away and transform it into something so much more powerful than anything that had been done to her. I wish she could have known how many firefighters would one day stand on their feet and clap for her because she didn't let this moment be the end. And I wish she could have known that even before she found her ferocity, her story was worthy of being seen and she was worthy of being believed.

Trauma isn't just The Event—the fire, the assault, the shooting, the death, the divorce, the car accident. It's also what happens after. How quickly could you make yourself safe? Did people believe you? Did anyone blame you? Did you have access to medical care? Mental health support? Were the people close to you willing to walk with you through the recovery process? What was your life like before The Event? Did you grow up around people who met your needs? Did they validate you? Did they model positive ways to deal with stress? All of these factors and so many more dictate our initial response to a traumatic event and the way we carry it, the way we overcome it. If you constantly have to justify your hurt, then the part of you that's hurt is constantly and primarily searching to be understood and validated. That's where all your energy goes.

And overcoming the hurt doesn't mean you never feel it again. It just means that when you feel it, you don't stop there. It means that the pain no longer overwhelms you.

In that environment, my journals were the only place where I was recording the full truth about what was actually happening to me. I thought that if I wrote the truth down, no one could take it away from me. I thought that if I wrote it all down from the beginning, every single conversation and interaction, then I could see the signs that I must have missed and then never miss them again. I think of how often I've heard that sentiment from the hundreds of trauma survivors I've met since becoming one myself.

"I should have known what he was going to turn out to be."

"I knew that she was drunk and that nothing good was going to come of seeing her that night. I shouldn't have responded to her text and agreed to meet."

"That call sounded really bad when it was dispatched, and I knew that seeing a child hurt could affect me since I had a newborn at home. I shouldn't have gone to it."

I have been asked, "Why did you join that fire company if you knew that was going to happen?" (I didn't.) Another one I've heard is "I just don't understand why you let those things happen to you." (Imagine my disgust when a firefighter said this to me over burgers at a firefighting conference.) People need to find a way to fit your experience into their worldview, or into their "paradigm," as author Stephen Covey calls it. In the case of sexual harassment, assault, or violence, many people are quick to place blame on the victim rather than the choice someone made to harm.

Those questions are clearly founded in ignorance, but they can plant a seed in our mind that society waters. We might even water it ourselves. We want to find a place to lay our blame and find fault. Often it's easier to lay it on the closest and most accessible target: ourselves. We think we must have been at least complicit by putting ourselves in a vulnerable position. Or in the case of nonrelational trauma like experiencing a car accident, a random act of violence, or an act of mass violence, we still might try to find one piece of the puzzle to put on our shoulders.

And so we add shame on top of our hurt, and that shame becomes a layer that hardens over time, making the hurt and therefore the overcoming harder to access.

I want you to know what teenage Ali didn't: that expecting people to be good and trustworthy doesn't make you responsible for their shortcomings. Someone choosing to act in a way that harms you isn't a result of anything that you've done or any part of who you are. Not seeing trauma coming doesn't mean you are in any way responsible for it. Showing up for someone, whether that's on an emergency scene or in a relationship, doesn't mean that blame for other people's choices belongs anywhere near your shoulders. I've spent a lot of time thinking about what it means to forgive, and I realized that forgiveness has to start with yourself. It was the first and I think biggest step for me. Forgive yourself for not having a crystal ball, forgive yourself for trusting someone who eventually harmed you, forgive yourself for returning to the place of trauma or staying in it too long. Forgive yourself.

REFLECTION AND ACTION

Truth #1 for Overcoming:
Forgive Yourself for Not Seeing It Coming

If you told the story of what happened to you to someone who deeply cared about you, what would they say? If you could have received comfort and validation at the time, what would that have sounded like? It's never too late to give ourselves what we need. Write it down, perhaps in the form of a letter of forgiveness to yourself. Acknowledge that no matter the circumstances or outside factors, you were not complicit in your trauma. Say it or write it to yourself until it feels true.

2

WORK TO FIND COHERENCE IN YOUR LIFE STORY

What a comfort to know that God is a poet.
—*Rachel Held Evans*

On May 31, 1889, human negligence coupled with an ungodly amount of rain caused the man-made South Fork Dam to burst. Twenty million gallons of water hemorrhaged out of Lake Conemaugh and quickly drained into the valley below. The "terrible wave" traveled down through the mountain with the force of Niagara Falls, picking up buildings and horses, locomotives and barbed wire, a seventy-five-foot-tall viaduct, and human beings alive, dead, and dying. One hour after the dam let go and fourteen miles later, the wave finally hit Johnstown, Pennsylvania, at ninety miles per hour and killed 1 out of every 9—over 2,200 people. As the water hit the mountain to the north of downtown Johnstown and finally settled, the debris gathered at the stone bridge and then caught fire, burning as many as five hundred people alive. The fire would burn for two days until the Pittsburgh Fire Department arrived by train to put it out.

I first heard of the Johnstown Flood on a seventh-grade field trip. My classmates and I stood near the spot where, on the morning of the flood, workers stood in the driving rain atop the dam, frantically trying to stop the inevitable. On the bus ride home that day, I sat silently, mesmerized by the choices people had made during and right after the flood. At the sight or sound of what was coming, some ran. Some froze. Some reached back to help others up a hill or pull them into attics. Others pushed people out of the way to get ahead of them. Some picked up those who couldn't run only to drop them to their death after realizing they only had the energy to save themselves. After looking toward an unfamiliar noise and seeing the tops of the trees bending toward him, engineer John Hess said to his coworkers, "The lake's broke," and ran his number 1124 train backward toward the doomed town, tying the whistle down to scream a warning to anyone who could hear it.

If they survived the initial impact, people grabbed ahold of anything that would float. A woman clung to her roof rafters while every single one of her children drowned around her. Family members clung to each other in trees, naked, as the violence of the impact had stripped them bare. As they balanced on pieces of lumber, fathers tossed their babies to anyone standing on solid ground. Some, as soon as they found dry land, started walking in an unknown direction and didn't stop until they were found days later by people who were coming into town to help. That night, with no medical supplies or light, a doctor with broken ribs delivered two babies on the upper floor of Alma Hall. Two hundred sixty-four stunned survivors shivered there that night, praying out loud that the building would not catch on fire or break apart around them. Those two babies would be given the first name "Flood."

Five days later, Clara Barton arrived, having recently established the American branch of the International Red Cross. While tending to those in town, she noted "a profound melancholia" among survivors, "associated with an absolute disregard of the future." Yet it was the belief of the men put in charge that "there was no sense dwelling on the thing" and that doing so was "bad for the spirits."

Whether or not we want to, we dwell. Trauma sits in our minds and demands to be dealt with. After I visited Johnstown in seventh grade, I understood trauma as something that came in the form of a destructive mass of water and earth. In eleventh grade, I began experiencing it at the hands of other people's words and actions, but I didn't know that counted as trauma too. After my own trauma experiences, almost unknowingly, I began searching for more stories of survival like those I'd first learned of in Johnstown. On days when I had the time, I would find myself at the library. I never had a specific title I was looking for, but I would always end up in front of the same rack of books: the survivors.

I stood in the shadowed quiet of the massive library and waited, like a secret was about to be revealed to only me. My eyes patiently skimmed the vertical spines until, suddenly, a title would catch my eye and I would feel like those who survived were standing before me. They were soldiers, first responders, Holocaust heroes, survivors of every kind of loss, of all the kinds of pain we inflict on ourselves and each other. I read those stories because I wanted to know how many ways there were to "get it back." How far did they fall? Did their pain look like mine? Did we feel it the same way? How did you find a way to pull your pieces back together and decide to continue on?

I became really good at separating that painful part of my life from everything else. Compartmentalizing was the beginning of my brain attempting to cauterize the wound to keep the toxicity from spreading to the rest of my life. I was desperate for some relief. Each week, I went to the firehouse at a designated time for my shift, praying that there would be a call so I could help someone in need. While I was there, I would figuratively close my eyes so I wouldn't be overcome by the dark, and then when I got back to the safety of my house, I could open my eyes again.

In high school, all I wanted was to find a group of people that I fit in with. I wanted to find those who also felt Big Feelings, who also saw the world through the lens of melodies and imagination. I found it in the high school theater club. Aside from my house, high school theater was my safest place. It was a place where people stepped onstage in someone else's clothing to tell someone else's story. Onstage, everyone acted in ways that I could understand and in ways that were predictable. Onstage, the words *lights up* and *end scene* signaled the open and the close. I could see pain or trauma coming because it was written into the script and got resolved by the time the curtain fell. Then the actors would come up to the front of the stage for curtain call smiling, free of the strife in the stories they had just lived. There were no leftover hardships, no carried-over pains, no ripples. I loved the order of it, the simplicity of it, the magic of it. I felt a shielded protection when I was telling other people's stories. I didn't have to think about the story I was actively living, the one I did not yet have words for.

The old auditorium building sat in a big dip in the earth, so much so that during periods of heavy rain, we would see the water start to seep in along the front of the stage and slowly creep up to the first row of seats. I remember running back to the band room in the middle of rehearsal with my friend Amber to pick the clarinets and trumpets up out of the rising water. I'm grateful for the theater and the refuge it gave me and so many other kids. At a time in my life when so much was out of my control, the theater stayed safe, whole, and predictable. A brand-new school building sits there now, with a new auditorium that does not flood. I wish I'd found a way to go sit in the old theater one more time before they tore it down.

Despite the respite I found in the theater, all I wanted was to leave that town. Finally, high school graduation festivities were underway, but I felt shackled to this secret war I was fighting alone. How was I supposed to explain this all to my classmates, to my friends? They wanted to talk about boys and college; I was distracted by the fatal car accident I'd seen the night before and the hideous comment that was made to me while I cleaned the blood off my gear. I wanted to ask other girls, "Do you know about this damn cage? Do you know what happens if you refuse it?" I rode the rides at Hershey Park during Senior Skip Day and smiled in the pictures, but I was still tethered to the fire station, where the floor smelled like diesel fuel and wet hose, where my safety was never guaranteed, where we played by rules in a game I didn't understand.

I began to have dreams that weren't events so much as a feeling—the feeling of helplessness. One centered on what happened during my first hazmat certification. Very few certifications are mandated in the American Fire Service. The federal government leaves it up to each state to determine what training you need to be a firefighter. A lot of states have no training requirements. As a result, unless your state or specific firehouse has decided you need to meet certain standards in order to be a firefighter, you can go into the most dangerous emergency situations with very little to no training. However, there is one federally mandated certification— for handling hazardous materials—and you have to recertify in this training annually. Like most standardized certifications, there is a written test and a skills test. The written test is scored, but each skill station is a "pass/fail."

During my first hazmat skills test, I was called away from the rest of the group. I figured maybe there was an individual station they were surprising us with, which isn't unheard of. I followed the instructor who had beckoned me until we got to the other side of the lot, out of earshot from anyone else. He gestured to the charged hose line that was laying there in the dirt.

"Self-decon," he stated flatly.

Self-decon? This wasn't a skill I'd been prepared for. I wracked my brain, going over the pages of notes, the multiple books I'd read in preparation, the Power-Point slides I'd studied. Self-decon? I was stumped until I looked—really looked—at the instructor's face. His eyes, deviant. His mouth, smirking. *Oh. I get it.*

I picked up the hose line and held the nozzle over my head. I squeezed the trigger just long enough for a burst of water to be expelled and then immediately let off the pressure. I stared at him. He stared at me. His eyes went to my chest. I felt defiant in realizing that it was covered with my bulky fire coat. Water dripped down my face and into my eyes, but I did not move. We stood in a standoff. I briefly considered turning away and running, but after a few moments, he smirked again. "Pass," he said as if he hadn't made up a fake skill just for me. He walked away disinterested, like a dog done playing with a toy. I turned around and realized just how far we'd walked away from the group, how alone I'd been. That night, I dreamed that I was alone in a giant black void, soaking wet, water dripping into my eyes. I was screaming for someone to hear me, but no one ever came.

At the time, I didn't know the significance of things that show up in our dreams. In my work with first responders these days, I often hear panic when they tell me that sights or sounds from memorable calls are showing up in their dreams. Same thing with survivors of interpersonal violence or abuse or those who have survived a near-death accident. It could be a smell, a sound, or a sight that keeps showing up. Maybe it's the feeling of panic or fear. We might even try to avoid sleep for fear of experiencing the trigger. What shows up in our dreams is informing us that part of the experience is asking for more attention. Your brain is doing every-thing it possibly can to process and find coherence in these experiences, and if you aren't allowing it time and space to process when you're awake, your unconscious mind will attempt to jump-start the process. While it definitely feels jarring, it is a good sign because (1) it tells you that your brain knows that work needs to be done and (2) it tells you where to start. Memories come up like this to tell us where we can start our coherence work.

But our brains are incredibly resilient and magnifi-cently flexible. Our brains literally "livewire," as David Eagleman says. This means that our brains are not stag-nant or fully formed when we are born but grow and change throughout our lives as the demands we put on them change. In Eagleman's book *Livewired*, he tells us that "the brain chronically adjusts itself to reflect its challenges and goals. It molds its resources to match the requirements of its circumstance. When it doesn't pos-sess what it needs, it sculpts it." This is great news for trauma recovery, as it means that we are perpetually and immediately able to work toward the coherence of our life stories and that our brains will create new space for our growth.

Looking back at myself during this time in my life, I think that, more than anything, I needed to know that my belief in the goodness of the fire service wasn't mis-placed, that the missing-piece feeling I'd had at the start wasn't wrong. I needed to know that I was just unlucky to have found such a shitty firehouse environment in my hometown and that these experiences were not indicative of the fire service as a whole.

By the time I graduated high school in 2007, I felt like I'd lived a decade of life in the last three years. I decided to take a year off between high school and college. I was searching but still tethered. I felt that if I walked away, they would win. I can look back with empathy for my younger self and see my focus on winning and losing as a sign of my young age. I was being hurt to the point of being traumatized, and "winning" would have been knowing when to walk away—not for them but for me, for my quality of life.

I was spending less time at the firehouse and only responding to calls when there was a common goal we could all rally around and focus on. I needed to know that firefighting was still possible for me. Then one day, I found what felt like an answer. My mom read an interview that the chief of the San Francisco Fire Department had done with *Time* magazine. This was such a big deal because the chief was a woman. I wrote her an email, reaching for a lifeline.

I told her a bit about me and my experiences in the fire service and told her that the only thing keeping me going was faith in myself. I asked for any advice she could offer. A few days later, I sat on a stool in my dad's workshop with a yellow pad of legal paper in front of me. The chief had responded to my email and wanted to talk on the phone. I had questions I wanted to ask her written out so I wouldn't forget or trip over my words. During our phone call, she told me that if I could get myself to San Francisco, they would put me up for a week and that I would meet every female firefighter she could put in front of me. That June, I found myself on a plane heading west.

I was picked up at the airport in a fancy San Francisco Fire Department SUV by a kind firefighter named Mindy. From the second I landed, I felt welcomed and safe. Mindy took me to lunch and then drove me to the department's headquarters. I met the receptionist I'd initially emailed and was then welcomed into the fire chief's office. Stepping into that room felt like a dream. She gave me some San Francisco Fire shirts and a blanket that I still have. We sat and talked, just the two of us female firefighters. I remember the gold on her uniform shirt, her ponytail, her smile.

Mindy then dropped me off at the townhouse I'd be staying in. A firefighter and her wife owned the house, and the entire top floor was an empty apartment. Molly, the firefighter's wife, gave me a copy of the book she had edited called *Hard Hatted Women*.

Her inscription read, "For Ali, part of a new generation of pioneers. Keep up the good fight. You are great! June, 2008." I felt seen. That book still sits prominently on my bookshelf.

I was driven around the city, welcomed into firehouses as if I belonged there, and given hugs and high fives and smiles. I cooked dinner alongside firefighters, rode in the trucks alongside them, grocery shopped, and performed hydrant maintenance with them. There were women firefighters everywhere, in every position and rank. Adult Ali knows that no work environment is perfect, but sixteen-year-old Ali felt that this was the most perfect fire department in the world. It was the complete antithesis to everything I'd experienced up until that point. It was my answered prayer. I've never been scared of the job, but I have been afraid of those I did that job with. In this city, for the first time, I stood in a firehouse and didn't feel fear.

In the evening, we sat around a giant, round kitchen table, assembling and devouring tacos whose ingredients spun on the massive lazy Susan in front of us. I sat next to a woman firefighter who I'd been hanging out with all day. Earlier, I'd helped her study for her lieutenant exam by googling pictures of structures that were on fire and asking her to give me a size-up report as if she was arriving first on the scene of a fire and had to give a concise report to all incoming units. She is now a battalion chief. That night at dinner, I watched her effortlessly move through the conversations that were going on around us. She was funny, kind, at home, and in charge.

On my third day in the city, I was taken to Station 35, which sits on the shore of San Francisco Bay. I was given a tour of the nautical-themed station and then led outside by one of the acting chiefs. I followed him out of the back of the station while looking down at my camera, eager to capture every moment of this life-affirming trip. He paused, holding the door open for me, and when I looked up, the sight truly took my breath away. I raised my camera and snapped a picture. San Francisco Station 35 holds two fireboats, the *Phoenix* and the *Guardian*. There they sat in front of me, floating in the blue water, docked under the Bay Bridge. Purple flowers decorated the dock, and deck chairs sat overlooking the water. The water shone and sea gulls flew overhead. I heard laughs coming from inside the station. All was well.

The chief had arranged for me to take a boat ride. With a San Francisco Fire Department coat wrapped around my shoulders, I looked out over the bay. The first female fireboat captain in the history of the department was at the helm. The Golden Gate Bridge was in the distance. As we wound our way around Alcatraz, the other firefighters let me know how much they appreciated me coming to visit. Those moments on the *Guardian* were the safest and most free I'd felt since joining the fire service.

This experience furthered the dichotomy that the fire service would continue to hold for me. In this world, I would have to fight off an attempted gang rape *and* I would be welcomed in with open arms. It was an *and*, not an *or*. *And*.

Those firefighters were a big part of the reason I didn't just quit. I went back home, energized but unsure of how to proceed in my own life. I now knew good and safe firehouses existed. Before going to San Francisco, I'd been so sad at the reality of my own firehouse. A part of me thought maybe these firefighters didn't know any better, maybe they were just ignorant. Maybe they were just treating me the way they'd been taught to treat women. That attitude forgave their actions without them deserving it or asking for it. But mostly, it relieved me of expending the energy I didn't yet have. Feeling the necessary anger would have collapsed me at that point.

In an interview talking about her book *Strange Piece of Paradise*, author Terri Jentz calls this "an easy forgiveness . . . a kind of cheap grace." On a June night in 1977, Terri survived an attempted murder while she was camping with a friend. After, people would ask what happened to the man who drove his pickup truck onto their tent and hacked her arms with an ax, and she would say, "Oh, I didn't think much about him." This method of retelling the pain separate from the one who caused it was an act of self-preservation; it was telling her story in a sterile timeline, like I had. Looking back, Terri says, "It was tremendously detrimental because it left me with this legacy of powerlessness, of an inability to resume my will."

Decades later, she revisited the site of her attempted murder and laid down in the grass on the exact place where her life had almost been ended: "I felt like there was some part of my being, of my 19 year old self . . . and certainly my real blood had been left behind in that soil . . . I just instinctively dropped to my knees and laid down flat on the spot and soaked in the part of myself that had fled. And when I had her back I got up and I walked out of that park by myself." Terri describes her anger as something she needed to recover. Her numbed and stunted self was replaced by a "warrior woman" who launched her on a path to discover who had done this to her and, in turn, insert a power bigger than the trauma over The Event.

I needed to do the same, to return and collect the parts of me that had been taken away, but I simply was not yet ready. I needed to work toward coherence, toward finding connection through all these events and an overall consistency in my life story. After coming home from the West Coast, I realized how much of a choice it all was. These men were choosing to continue acting in a way that would hurt me. As soon as I drew my boundaries and they continued to cross them, they could no longer be excused as ignorant. The embers of rage smoldered somewhere deep, but I couldn't yet connect with the feeling that would eventually motivate me to take a big action.

After the three years I spent at that first firehouse, I finally went away to college to get the fire science degree I had always wanted. My experiences in San Francisco showed me that it was possible to find a good firehouse to do the job that I loved while also being safe. In my new college classes, professors would ask who had fire service experience—I would not raise my hand. I thought if I pretended that none of those experiences had happened, I could be a brand-new person without them. I thought I could just "move on" and "start fresh." The trauma had settled deep, the parts of me in pain were numb, and for the time being, ignoring it all allowed me to breathe.

I got settled into my new place and came across the plastic bin full of the journals I had filled during my first three years as a firefighter. I looked at those twenty-two journals—some spiral-bound, others covered with stickers or scribbled with quotes—and felt like I was staring at pieces of myself that had been forcibly removed from my body against my will. I felt led to open the first journal, a small, square, spiral-bound book with lined pages and a sun and moon on the front. I read about that first day wearing the fire gear that was two sizes too big, the feeling of being at home.

That day, I went through every single one of the journals. I ripped off pieces of a blue Post-it, putting little tabs on each page where something significant happened. I was walking back through those years of my life and picking up the breadcrumbs my younger self had scattered. Then I sat down at my brand-new laptop and started typing. I don't remember what those first words were, but as soon as I typed them, I knew that telling my story was important and something I wanted to see through. Every single day, *Where Hope Lives*, my first book, poured out of me. It was the beginning of me connecting with the parts of myself trauma had fractured, the first moment of me reclaiming these stories as mine. When it came to finding a title, I thought back to my first trip to San Francisco and that city. I wrote about the experience, saying, "In the city where hope lives, the sun is always shining." *Where Hope Lives*.

As I became aware of the significance of my story through writing *Where Hope Lives*, I began testing the waters by using my own voice to speak the truth in my college speech class. Every time I stood up and told little bits of my story and the ground did not open up and swallow me whole, I felt brave enough to tell more and more of it. I remember the first time I stood up in front of my class with a few pages of notes in front of me. I wish I could remember the words I'd used back then, but I'm sure if I could read them now, I would see my younger self laying the groundwork for what I do today.

Where Hope Lives was initially written about a girl named Haley. Everything I wrote about actually happened—I just wrote it as if it happened to this other girl. Separating myself from the events in the story helped me get enough perspective on them to tell the story. I also considered publishing the book under a pen name. But when I was ready, I used "find and replace" to swap Haley's name with mine. I figured that I couldn't write a story about standing up and being brave without putting my own name on it.

When I was getting ready to graduate from college, after having spent all those years rewriting those memories, I realized I had written a story that was not just about me. It wasn't solely about a girl in a firehouse in a tiny town. It was the first version of the story you are now reading, a tale of injustice and oppression, redemption and forgiveness, separation and wholeness. I thought about how I would've felt less alone if I'd had that book when I was struggling. And that in and of itself made me want to finish it.

In May 2010, I graduated with my associate's degree in fire science, and instead of continuing on to get another degree, I decided to follow my story. I moved back home to the town that held my bad memories, knowing I was going to have to face them if I wanted to move forward with this dream of turning *Where Hope Lives* into something people could hold in their hands.

I tried to get an agent and then a publishing company interested in *Where Hope Lives*, but everyone wanted to change it somehow. But changing even one thing would make the entire story untrue. One person in the industry even told me that they "loved the story" but planned to add vampires to it, as the Twilight franchise was exploding at the time. I said no to them all and decided to do it on my own.

I googled "How do you self-publish a book?" and printed out what I found. I moved back into my old room, got my old waitressing job back, started a second job as a barista at Starbucks, and began living life with one goal in mind: publishing my story. When I made that move home, I was feeling driven and full of purpose. But as I started to exist again in my hometown—a college town, a town full of people my age who had very specific life paths set in motion—the feeling How was I supposed to explain what I was living for?

"Hey, Ali, what are you doing with your life?" was always how I was greeted by people who had watched me grow up and knew that I was back in town.

I wanted to say, "I'm going to be the author of a bestselling book. I'm going to travel the world and tell people that it's OK not to fit inside someone else's expectations. That it's OK to stand up. That sometimes you have to in order to save yourself."

Each morning, I was serving coffee at Starbucks before the sun rose. After a few hours, I'd walk across the street, change out of my coffee-stained black uniform, and transform into a 1950s waitress: black dress with an apron, fire-engine-red lipstick, saddle shoes. Every dollar I made was going to help *Where Hope Lives* be born. At that time, I did not yet understand that I had been deeply changed from my time in firehouses or that my journey of overcoming trauma was not over. I'd taken the pain and buried it, but like the way your skin holds a splinter, it would come back to the surface eventually. I was sharing the parts of my story that I was able to, unaware that there was much more work to do before I could tell it completely.

I had no idea what I was going to do after publishing the book or what I wanted the rest of my life to look like. But I knew that if I could keep following that story, if I could keep being the person who was brave enough to live through it and then tell it, I would always find my way. As I was finishing the book, I was often worried that I was going to forget to say something important. I thought that *Where Hope Lives* would be the only big thing I was ever able to say. At this point, the book had been done for a while and had been professionally edited more than once, but I was still in the Word document every day. I reached out to Jodi Picoult, one of my favorite authors, to see if she had any advice. Miraculously, she responded with advice that I lean on every single time I am approaching the end of a writing project: "When you would change less than 2% of it, it's done."

In December 2010, a cardboard box arrived at my house: the very first copies of *Where Hope Lives*. I'd heard rumors that someone from that first fire company was going to try to "steal a copy," so I picked up the first copy of it I'd ever held and walked it straight to the current fire chief's house. He looked confused and defensive as he opened the door. I smiled disarmingly and put the book in his hands, figuring if he wanted to talk about the book, he might as well read it. He and I were both surprised at my audacity to be standing there.

The next night, I was working the closing shift at Starbucks. I always dreaded being in that town at night, among the bars and restaurants, among the drunk and drinking. The smell of alcohol threatened to dislodge a memory from my brain. That deep-seated trigger was beginning to show. I was starting to avoid situations where I might have a response. Looking back, I can see how much shame I had piled on top of that, a very normal reaction to what I had experienced. It would be years before I understood that triggers aren't to be feared but, like dreams, simply provide us with information about where there is work to be done. I can see how the shame was a barrier that kept me from feeling anything else. I think of the quote from Liz Plank's *For the Love of Men*: "Shame is not just a feeling; it's a barrier to functioning."

Triggers are overwhelming and can be really frustrating. They can be like stepping in mental quicksand. As you react to whatever caused the trigger, your brain thinks you are back in the trauma instead of the memory of it. Triggers can feel like our bodies are having a reaction that we are not choosing to be a part of yet get consumed by. Instead of feeling anger at a trigger for coming up or at yourself for not being able to suppress it, I encourage you to talk to the younger version of yourself. Our younger selves are still in us and will continue to cry out until we give them the comfort they deserve. I learned how to greet my triggers when they surfaced. If I found myself feeling scared because I was standing with my back to a wall with no way out directly behind me, I'd say, "Hey, trigger, thank you for keeping me safe for so long. I appreciate you. But we are safe now. And I don't need you anymore."

When we're triggered, we need something that can pull us to a place of mental safety instead of a place of fear. I call it an anchor. Your anchor could be a thought or a mantra like "I am safe in my body" or "No matter what others do, I have the ability to make decisions that are best for me." It could be a song, poem, or prayer. It could be a memory of your happiest moment or of something else you have overcome. It's anything that grounds you to the present moment and moves your thoughts from a place of fear to a place of stability.

After learning of *Where Hope Lives*, the college I'd graduated from invited me to come back and speak. For the first time, I stood on a stage in the room where I'd studied building construction while my old classmates sat in the seats facing me. I talked about living my story, and the words I would use in the years to come were beginning to emerge. I talked about the long hours of work and why I felt so motivated to share the story of what happened to me. It felt electric, like the beginning of something. I decided then that I was going to take every opportunity I could to get my story in front of an audience, any audience, no matter the size. I started to travel, stand on stages, and remind myself—and the audience—that we are the only ones who have a say in how our stories go. I sold my book in states I had previously never been to. I heard from readers who I'd never met. I realized that owning the power of *Where Hope Lives* meant that I was no longer voiceless. But the existence of *Where Hope Lives* gave me another quality that would forever make me stand out in emergency services. I was always going to be known in firehouses first as "the girl who wrote that book." I was going to have to bear the consequence of standing up for the rest of my life, for as long as my book existed. I made as much peace with that as I could, as I felt the good it could do in the world was worth it.

After one of those first speaking engagements ended, I drove home through the quiet night. Nothing but the music and the moon accompanied me, the moon riding high over my left shoulder as I passed the truck stops and strip clubs. As I crossed the Susquehanna River and got one mile closer to home, the moon slid to my right. Illuminated, the clouds looked broken, like a shattered mirror, and the stars watched me from their light-years away. The music I played, Justin Nozuka and Sara Bareilles, carried me, holding me up until I could finally rest.

When I pulled into my sleeping town, I looked at my first firehouse. There was no need to check in on it anymore, but I knew I always would. Even now, I look to see if the lights are on, if the bay doors are up, if any of the trucks are out on a call. It used to feel like parts of me died there—the parts of me that believed in the goodness of people and had the ability to trust others and herself. Part of the burying and avoiding I was doing at the time meant I stopped looking for that person and accepted that she was gone.

Nevertheless, I had a strong desire to return to the fire service. I still loved many parts of it, but I also now know I was experiencing what's called "trauma mastery"—when someone returns to an abusive situation like I did, not because they are weak or want to be abused, but because they desperately want a different outcome. We don't want the trauma to be The End. But too often, the situation we return to has not changed, and the abusers have no awareness of the work we've done or even of the simple fact that they are being abusive. So the same thing happens again and again, and this just reinforces and compounds the original hurt and deepens our response to it.

This repetition causes us to feel powerless over our lives and can lead us to feel how I used to: *I was put on this earth to be other people's victim. There's nothing I can do about it. I should just accept it.* I remember the lightbulb that came on when, while earning my psychology degree, I read about a mental state called "learned helplessness." This happens over time when we continuously face a "negative and uncontrollable circumstance" and therefore begin to feel that we are powerless to affect any change over it, so we simply stop trying. My experiences in firehouses taught it to me. I struggled with it for a long time.

I joined a new firehouse ninety minutes away from my hometown, thinking that it would be too far for anyone to know who I was. But every time I began the drive there, my stomach would turn and my pulse would race. I always felt really nauseated when I walked in the door, and I felt like I relaxed only when I was on my way home again. I did not know that my body was reacting to a trigger. I had no idea that being in a firehouse was continuing to traumatize me, continuing to add droplets to my bucket of cumulative stress, continuing to teach my brain and body that I never knew where I was going to be safe. But I was standing on a fragile faith that I was going to be OK there. I was trying to beat into my head that the reference points to fear were no longer accurate, but sheer willpower is not enough to unlearn what trauma has taught us to be afraid of.

One day, after running a few calls, a lieutenant asked to speak with me in the chief's office. He sat me down and spoke cautiously: "The guys here, they've been hearing some things said about you and... they just don't feel... that they want to work with you. . . . They won't work with you."

I stared at him blankly, mute, stunned.

He cleared his throat uncomfortably, searching for clarity: "Apparently you've got a bad reputation from your first firehouse, and it seems that reputation has spread here." It makes sense now. When abusers can longer control you through their actions, when you remove yourself from their presence, they attempt to control you through what other people think of you.

At that moment, I felt the ground fall away. The fragile faith I'd been clinging to was obliterated. I saw myself walking around the giant warehouse of my mind and systematically shutting off lights. I went dark, mentally scrambling for safety. In the years since that conversation, I wish I'd had the presence of mind to ask what specifically was being said. I wish I could have known exactly what apocryphal tale he'd heard: I wish I'd been this adult version of myself. I don't remember if I said anything to him at the time. Probably "I'm sorry." For what, I don't know.

I drove home in silence. I began to feel a strong disconnect, the split that trauma causes, like there were two halves of me. I looked down at my white-knuckled hands on the steering wheel and felt like they belonged to someone else. There was a seed planted in my mind, one that began to grow as it was watered by my exit from that second firehouse. I was done there. I could never go back. I felt like I should have said goodbye to someone, but I couldn't think of who. I was reading *Where Hope Lives* a lot during this time, seeing the answer in black and white. I'd written words that, at the time, I didn't fully comprehend. In my hands, I held a completed book but an unfinished story. I felt that I needed to go back to that town, to the place that held all of my trauma, and try to get a different outcome.

I can see now how much I missed out during that time in my life because I was so busy grappling with the cage and the consequences of refusing it. It's risky to love something so much because losing it also means losing the parts of yourself that loved it. I was so consumed with the love I had for firefighting, and protecting that love took everything I had. To eventually overcome it, I needed to be sad about that for a while. While experiencing trauma, we miss out on feeling safe, on trusting others, on trusting the world around us. We miss out on trusting ourselves. This can cause a pain that sits deep and a grieving that is an important part of climbing out of the valley. It wasn't just changing the circumstances of my life that eventually helped me find my After, but an active acknowledgment of what I wasn't able to do or be at the time of my trauma. We might avoid the full reality of what we have experienced for a long time. I thought that only allowing myself to feel parts of my story—a little grief here, a little anger there—was enough to satisfy the parts of me that were craving an acknowledgment for the pain I'd live through. We need to look at the entirety, at all the events that have made us who we are. Finding coherence is what allows us to keep moving forward.

REFLECTION AND ACTION

Truth #2 for Overcoming:
Work to Find Coherence in Your Life Story

Is there a part of your life's story you have yet to say out loud? Is there an experience you haven't been able to rectify in your mind? Are there experiences you missed out on while you were busy surviving? Allow yourself time to acknowledge and then grieve those losses. It doesn't take away from where you are now. Was there an event that impacted you in ways you haven't fully acknowledged to yourself? Gently challenge yourself to see around any shame you might have attached to these experiences—it does not belong on your shoulders. I invite you to make a timeline of your life to literally see that the difficult periods did not end you. The version of yourself reading this right now is *alive*, and that is solid enough of a foundation to begin again. Write out your timeline or think it through until it's clear.

3

YOUR STRUGGLE IS
A TUNNEL, NOT A CAVE

*Even when the rain falls, even when the flood starts
 rising,
even when the storm comes, I am washed by the water.*
                              —*NEEDTOBREATHE*

As I set my sights on joining my third firehouse, one
that was four miles away from my first, trouble started.
Firefighters from my first firehouse were trying to ensure
I never got to call another firehouse home. It had been
years since we were colleagues, but as soon as I resur-
faced and "dared" to want to rejoin the fire service, my
presence aggravated that old wound. But the fire chief
of this new station took an action I'd stopped expecting from people. He went to these people, these trouble-
makers, and told them, "This stops now. She is with us.

You don't get to do this anymore." Because of this huge step, this man's choice to publicly and vocally be on my side, to have the awareness of everything I'd endured in my first firehouse and take an action to draw the finish line, I believed the war was won.

After submitting my application to join, I sat down for an interview in front of three firefighters who asked me the question I was expecting: "We don't have any other females here. How will you handle that?"

I should have asked them how they were going to handle it, but I didn't have those words at the time. I gave some answers about this not being my first rodeo and made them laugh to defuse the tension they'd created. I was always doing that, trying to make it easier for others to be in my presence. Those men agreed that I could join their firehouse and then walked me to the gear room to get fitted. I instinctively asked for shirts that were a size large, even though I can fit into a size small.

A few days later, my first call with this new firehouse came. I arrived at the station as the "box was placed available," which meant the emergency was over and the fire department was not needed. I walked up the bay between the two fire trucks and glanced down to see the red reflected in the puddles on the concrete floor. The rain had been pouring down in heavy sheets, creating the puddles inside, and a fine mist sprayed in like a breeze off the ocean. I was wearing jeans and an oversized sweatshirt, but in that environment, I felt completely naked and exposed. My neck felt like it was being squeezed, but I just pulled my collar away from it and kept walking.

As I got closer to the group of firefighters at the front of the bay, a gaggle of female college students walked past. The firefighters made the usual vulgar remarks, gestures, and catcalls. I looked down at my body, wondering what they said about me when I wasn't there to hear it. Then I flashed back to a memory from my first firehouse: As I walked inside one night, I was greeted by the sight of everyone wearing sunglasses. I jokingly asked if the lights were too bright, only to be mocked with smirks.

"They're on so we can look at you wherever we want."

Standing in the new firehouse that night, I fought the urge to cross my arms across my chest. I was trying to take responsibility for my life by showing up in places I wanted to be. That's all I thought I had control over, and for a while, it felt like it was working. I had my first training at this new firehouse the following week. The training required us to be "on air" and breathe through the face mask connected to the air cylinder on our backs. As the man in charge of the training gave us instructions, I went on air to make sure there was actually air in the cylinder in case someone had purposefully emptied it. The man running the training turned to me.

"Please disconnect your air, Ali."

My finger found the big release button, pressed it, and then turned the regulator counterclockwise to disconnect it from my mask.

"I know it's only two or three breaths until you go into the smoke trailer, but in a real fire, if something has gone wrong, those breaths could keep you alive or at least keep you conscious until we can come in to get you."

I looked at him curiously through the plastic of my face piece. He looked back at me. I realized that he would come in to save me if I needed him to.

This experience gave me the assurance I needed to allow other firefighters to get close enough to become friends. This included two college-aged guys, one I nicknamed Charlie Brown (or "CB") and another named Forrest, who was usually told, "Run, Forrest, run."

That weekend we went to the local fire academy to run practical drills. We all converged on the fire floor; two hoses, one red and one green, lay charged with water side by side. High-rise packs and spare rolls of hose were thrown to the floor, and we readied ourselves to advance to the "fire room," which was just a room with a giant orange traffic cone in it.

All of the sudden, one of the chiefs appeared behind us. He kicked our boots and yelled, "Evacuate! Evacuate! Get out now!" He disappeared back down the stairs. Less experienced firefighters looked around, confused at this common training tactic. Fire officers would let you get far enough into the evolution to make you think you've got it handled, then they'd come in with some fake catastrophe and disrupt everything to see what you'd do. Tools were left where they lay as we hoofed it down the stairs. Sweat clouded our face pieces.

"Come on, here we go!" we called out to each other as we hustled.

We tried not to trip over each other as we ran through the perfectly safe structure. As we came off the last flight of stairs and rounded the corner, a firefighter's massive hand came out of the shadows and grabbed me by the fabric of my coat. He deposited me behind him, where I was completely hidden by his Viking-sized frame. Another common training tactic: make someone disappear to see how long it would take the others to realize their team was not intact. In a real-world scenario, the faster you realize a firefighter is not with you, the faster you can find them, and the better chance you have at saving their life.

"You're lost," this firefighter told me, matter of fact. I stood silently behind him, playing along.

Charlie Brown came down off the stairs last and spotted me. He grabbed the shoulder strap on my air pack and pulled me with him.

"No!" Charlie Brown shouted firmly, muffled from behind his face piece.

"She's found!"

With each positive experience, I spent more time at the fire station, feeling more confident with each training I completed and each call I ran. Each moment at the firehouse was a reminder of what I loved about firefighting, and I thought that I'd found the place where I could finally stop struggling. I thought that I had made it through the tunnel of my past and that this new station was me being out in the sunlight. But the early days in this station were simply a reprieve where I could catch my breath before beginning the last and final part of my journey to finally make it out.

Every fire company has its own set of two alert tones, and when the dispatcher activates them, our pagers alarm. But we're always already sprinting before the beeping begins. What's in my hands gets tossed, set down, or dropped. My body starts to move, almost independent of me.

Habit, muscle memory, instinct, purpose.

It doesn't matter what the dispatcher says—a tree across the roadway, a dwelling fire with flames showing, a car accident with entrapment, rollover, ejection, or fire—we're already running before we know what we're running to. And before my mind can comprehend the steps, I am on the fire truck as the siren winds up.

There were eleven of us in that probationary class. Four would graduate, including me. We were the lowest rung on the ladder in that station as rookies. When there was a call, we'd find ourselves competing for the same space on the engine, as usually only one of us was allowed to take up a valuable place on the fire truck. During the excitement of a call, we would ricochet off each other like repelling magnets, reaching for the sides of our lockers as we approached them. Our row of lockers was tucked in a corner of the apparatus bay, hidden behind a massive fire truck, with barely enough room to get your gear on. As we were all trying to get dressed and others ran up behind us, we would grunt a quick "Go ahead" to indicate *It's tight quarters back here, just squeeze through where you can.* We grabbed the obnoxiously blue helmets that granted us the nickname "The Smurfs" and fought every urge to run.

After one call when I just couldn't get to the station fast enough, I walked back to the rows of lockers to find a mess of haphazardly kicked-off shoes, pagers, discarded sweatshirts, keys, and cell phones. I kicked the pairs of shoes back to their respective owners and smiled. I knew that my existence in that firehouse was a quiet rebellion, but for the moment, I was at peace with the responsibility and hopeful for my future there. The burden of my experiences I carried alone, but I mistakenly thought that because they weren't still painfully present in my mind, they were off my shoulders. I didn't know that what I needed was to be gentle with myself, that my pain needed validating, that I needed time away from painful memories, that stepping back into this environment had me walking on a tightrope that was perched on top of a bomb. I wish I could go back and tell that girl, who was about to be pushed off that tightrope and fall headlong into a trigger-filled valley, that she would find her way out the other side eventually. I wish I could tell her to go easy on herself during the climb.

After another call, as we pulled back into town and drove past my first firehouse, it began to rain. After the air cylinders were full, masks were clean, and everything was put back together, I looked outside and noticed a magnificent rainbow, complete and whole, perfectly formed in the sky. I thought it was a promise of safety. I thought I found the place that was going to hold my redemption. Now I see that rainbow as a promise that no matter how dark things become, there will always be light somewhere. Just like how I can have grace for the version of myself that sat in that police car, I can think of the version of myself standing there looking at that rainbow and no longer feel anger that she didn't know she hadn't made her way out of the tunnel just yet.

Another training night came along, this time on car fires. As most do, this fire company acquired junk cars from the towing company, put hay bales in them, and lit them, giving us the opportunity to fight the fire. When it was my turn, I stepped off the engine to walk up to my partner.

Suddenly, I felt threatened and completely panicked. My body was remembering a memory that my mind wasn't aware of. I felt angry at and unsafe around the firefighters who stood around me. A distantly familiar rage. My throat throbbed. *Something is wrong*, I thought. I looked down at my gloved hands and felt like they belonged to someone else. That night, we finished the training and I performed well, but I was shaken by the emotion that had come up.

A few weeks later, Hurricane Sandy was bearing down on the East Coast. All firefighters had been asked to staff one of the three stations. Charlie Brown baked a shoofly pie, Rick shot zombie Shane on *The Walking Dead*, and I watched the sun fall farther out of the sky as we crept closer to nightfall. When it was time, I chose to fall asleep in a recliner, giving some excuse about the "uncomfortable beds." But the truth was that getting into a bed—being horizontal and vulnerable, being alone in the dark surrounded by firefighters—was a trigger I couldn't put words to yet, let alone conquer. It was just before midnight and the station had fallen silent, except for the rain. It howled and poured outside as the powerful wind blew everything sideways into the building. I could not stop my heart from pounding every time I closed my eyes. My stomach hurt; my neck throbbed. I stretched my body out along the length of the chair and then curled up under the thin blanket.

"It's OK," I told myself. "You can sleep here."

My eyes would eventually grow heavy, and my breathing would slow. But then my body would flood with adrenaline and my heart would pound, forcing me to start the calming process all over again. Eventually, the sun rose and I went home. I had no idea that when our brains have connected a past experience to form a trigger, that connection is something that has to be actively unlearned. I thought that powering through the trigger was the way to get rid of it.

A few weeks later, we were going through mayday drills. When a firefighter is lost, disoriented, or trapped in a fire, we are trained to call "mayday" over our radios. Those situations are understandably some of the most stressful you can encounter on a fireground, so we practice over and over how to remain calm to conserve our air and communicate exactly where we are. Firefighters wear something called a Flash hood, similar to a ski mask but made of fire-resistant materials, to protect the face, neck, and ears—whatever's not covered by the helmet and mask. In this drill, we put the hood on backward to black out our masks and purposefully disorient ourselves, then worked through the unknown obstacles they had set up in the truck bay. Forrest had gone a few turns before me and was now helping with the drill. I was feeling my way along the massive tire of a fire truck when suddenly Forrest toppled an aluminum chain-link fence over me, then laid on top of it.

"Forrest, get off!" I shouted, muffled behind my face piece and the flash hood that was shoved in there to block my vision.

"No! I'm a roof! Get me off of you!"

Other firefighters that had gone ahead of me had too easy of a time escaping from under the chain-link fence "roof" in this drill, so they had six-foot-tall, broad-shouldered Forrest lay on top of it to make the weight a bit heavier.

"You're too fucking heavy!" I yelled.

"So figure it out!" he shouted back.

I got my arms under me and pushed hard into the concrete floor, giving myself enough room to wiggle out. He smacked the bottom of my boot as I crawled my way through the rest of the drill.

"Good job, Al!"

It can feel like that as we make our way out of our tunnel, like we have barely enough room to squeeze our way out. Our shoulders scrape against the side, our lungs compress, our muscles strain for freedom. Take your rest when you can. Find others who can keep you company. Seek out stories of others who have made their way out. Give it as many tries as you need. Every failed attempt to make it out still counts. Every attempt is an opportunity to learn exactly how strong we are. And each attempt gets us closer and closer.

Later that week at the firehouse, the firefighters were reenacting a scene from the TV show *24*, ambushing each other and barreling in and out of a pickup truck's open door.

"Freeze!" Finger guns were drawn.

"No, you freeze, motherfucker!"

I laughed at them, comfortably leaning against the back of the engine. And then, all of the sudden, a rough hand was covering my eyes. Someone much taller than me grabbed my left arm, pinning it to my chest. The world stopped. My breath slowed. I became hyperfocused on this person who was pushed up against my back. I wondered if I could fight myself away. I wondered if anyone would care if I screamed.

I shoved back hard with my right elbow and caught a joking, well-meaning firefighter square in the ribs. He doubled over, wincing.

"Sorry . . . I'm sorry," I managed to choke out. I'd been planning to stay the night, but I hurried home, which is where the near-hyperventilation began.

I felt fingernails cutting into my throat. Rough hands on the skin of my stomach. I tried to shake it off and waited for the release of sleep that night, but it didn't come.

There was a group of college students who lived at the firehouse, a common occurrence in volunteer fire stations. College students can live there for free while earning their degree, paying for room and board by running fire calls and taking care of other tasks around the station. But at this station, the nighttime drunken debauchery of these firefighters created an unpredictable and unstable environment.

One night, I responded to a call that was over before I made it too far in the door. I walked into the kitchen to see if anyone else was around and found a firefighter snoring and passed out face down in a puddle of his own puke and pee, with one foot sticking out the door as if he had tripped coming in. Drunk firefighters in a firehouse at night. A massive trigger. I vowed to never walk into the station after dark again. It was behavior that was encouraged because, as it was told to me, "It was reminiscent of the good old days when women were only allowed in the firehouse to cook, clean, or visit the men."

I'd stepped back into just trying to blend in, even though refusing the cage and writing *Where Hope Lives* eliminated that possibility. My femininity was once again my albatross and was made to be a quality that others always shone a light on. I'd take off any jewelry before entering the firehouse; the center console of my car was littered with earrings. I never bent over with my back (butt) facing anyone while getting my gear on. I didn't redo my ponytail in front of a crowd because I had once been told that taking my hair down in front of a firefighter and "playing with it" before putting it back into my ponytail holder was "teasing him."

"How was he supposed to know that you weren't flirting with him?" I had been told. So I added it to the metaphorical list of the rules that seemed to apply only to me. The unspoken rules for me at this firehouse were simple:

1. Pretend not to hear the consistent barrage of sexist jokes and make no comment on the nonconsensual sex acts that are bragged about.

2. Retain my femininity at all costs and remember at all times that I am only there because the men find me entertaining.

One afternoon, I sat at the kitchen table at the station, playing on my phone. A handful of older firefighters stood shoulder to shoulder at a big picture window, unabashedly catcalling the barely legal college students who walked by on their way to class. These firefighter's young daughters sat coloring at the table next to me while the men talked loudly about what they would do if they ever got those nameless girls alone. They talked about their favorite porn stars, sex positions, and which celebrities they would have sex with.

"Would you look at the tits on that..." one whistled as a young woman passed.

On that. I mulled over his word choice in my mind. *That.* I turned toward the freckle-faced girl who was coloring next to me and asked her to tell me about her drawing so she wouldn't hear the words coming out of her father's mouth. I wondered if her father's friends would say the same things about her when she was older. Who would ask her for her stories? They used their daughters and wives as shields against the claim of sexism, as if being a father or husband and sexist were mutually exclusive.

Girl Scout troops would occasionally tour the fire station, and I was always asked to be around so they could "see" me. I was happy to be there with the girls but could never ignore the strange dichotomy. I was allowed to be visible and appreciated when others were watching so that the firehouse could keep up the illusion of inclusivity. But when it was just us, they were working furiously to make sure I never felt seen. An article about the fire station was published in the local paper titled "The Blazing Brotherhood." With my gender completely erased, I felt like I didn't exist there at all. I never lectured them on feminism, never argued with them. But they were holding the sexist system together with both hands, trying to inject as much misogyny as possible to counteract the mirror I was holding up in front of them.

In the fire service and other work environments, this behavior has been called "bullying" to make it more palatable and therefore easier to talk about. But it shouldn't be palatable. It shouldn't be easy to talk about it. We have to be uncomfortable if we're ever going to be motivated to make a change.

One day after some sort of a public event, a bunch of firefighters, their family members, and I stood in the kitchen around greasy pieces of pizza. Sexist "jokes" flew back and forth as I tried to carry on a conversation with Forrest and some other firefighter friends. One of the wives leaned toward me as she walked past, following her husband out the door. "I don't know how you do it," she whispered, nodding back to the group. It was equal parts condescension, awe, and pity.

Just like in my previous firehouses, I was reminded that my reaction to this environment was the problem, instead of the environment itself or the people who perpetuated it. The repetition of these dangerous ideals was like acid, further leeching me away from myself. It made me feel like I couldn't make it out of the tunnel because, according to them, it was my fault for being there in the first place. But despite the constant gender wars, there was one person I never had to fight. I never had to justify my existence or question my safety around Forrest. A few months earlier, while in the car with him, he said something that I knew would change the rest of my life.

"Just kidding," I said, backpedaling out of a bad joke I'd made at his expense. "You know I love ya."

He looked me square in the eyes, all sense of humor gone from his face.

"I love you too."

In a town whose trauma I could not get away from, here was this boy who saw it all and refused to leave me alone with it. I didn't even realize who he was becoming for me because it was just effortless. Prior to him, I stopped making plans that included anyone else. I felt that my life was simply too much to ask for someone to walk it with me. He began to very regularly tell me that he loved me, and after a while, I realized he wasn't joking. I was terrified of him and who he was becoming to me. I vowed to keep Forrest as a friend, no matter how we felt about each other. It would be too complicated, too messy, too scandalous.

But still, I wanted Hannah, my best friend in the world, to meet him. I wanted him to be in every part of my life. One day, after months of knowing this about him, it was suddenly uncomplicated to me. All our comfortable conversations, our life goals that matched up, the ways we championed and cherished each other, the way our friendship had begun and quickly stabilized. On July 1, 2013, he told me that he loved me for the millionth time, except I said it back this time and meant it with my entire being. Three years later to the day, we married.

Recently, I asked Forrest about our beginning. I looked at the silver band I'd placed on his left ring finger while standing in front of our family and friends. He sat across from me at our kitchen table eating chicken on a fork, just like he used to during his college days. I reminded him of those dark days, explaining how I never expected someone like him to come along. I asked him how he knew I could get better, as he was there when I was in my mental valley. He shrugged.

"I just loved you through it."

I always felt that asking someone to move through life with me would be too much of a burden for them, but I never had to ask Forrest. He was simply there during the worst storm of my life while I thought I was at my most "difficult" and "challenging." But to him, the solution was neither. The answer was love. Not in the romantic, metaphorical sense—it was love through presence and love through action.

Forrest had a polar opposite experience in this firehouse. He experienced those men as helpful people who were interested in teaching him how to be a good firefighter and wanted to see him succeed. I experienced the same men as casual sexists who were content to look the other way when a true misogynist joined their ranks. Neither of us is wrong when we reflect back on that time in completely different ways. In those situations, it can be even harder to tell your story because other people could ask, "What are you talking about? He's such a nice guy." And he is, to that person. But not to everyone.

If you're met with the "but he's such a nice guy" comment when telling the truth about your experiences, I'm genuinely so sorry. I wish I could be there in that moment to help blunt the pain of that response. That response is due to that person not being able to hold your truth because it doesn't fit into their worldview, not because your truth is wrong.

I was actively searching for the good, for reasons to stay. I'd gotten a job as an EMT on the local ambulance and really enjoyed that work. One day, we were dispatched for a vehicle accident with ejection. This means that while the car was crashing, someone had been flung from it. (Wear your seat belt!) We arrived on the scene to find a car in a cornfield and the driver who had broken his pelvis in twenty-seven places. He crawled out of the cornfield toward the emergency vehicles.

"I was just really sad today," he told us quietly as we hurried over his broken body, realizing that the "accident" and his lack of a seat belt were intentional choices. The medic pumped him full of morphine—a mercy. During a pause in my EMT tasks, I watched the paramedic move over our patient in a practiced dance. It's one of my favorite things to notice on the scene of traumatic calls. You catch it in the moments between, in between getting the bag valve mask and unwrapping gauze, right after attaching the EKG nodes and spiking the IV bag. I love to watch people who are really good at what they do, and it's especially special to watch in situations that would overwhelm most.

Once at the trauma center, I moved aside to let the trauma chaplain into the trauma bay where the patient lay. We'd cut his clothes away to expose all possible wounds, and his waist was draped with a sterile, white blanket. I knew his pelvis was badly broken. I knew he would need to learn to walk again, to sit, to stand, to run. As the door closed, I watched the trauma chaplain stand over him, take his hand, and whisper a comforting word. I wondered how long the recovery process would be. How long would it take for him to want to get behind the wheel again? When he enters his After, what would he make of that night?

A few years ago, a trauma chaplain named James sat across from me at my kitchen table in Philadelphia and began to tell me what he's learned about what After looks like to him. James taught me that we always have company as we make our way through the tunnel. With a grin, he told me that, even though many trauma chaplains have wonderful call stories, their reasons for doing what they do, his were more like a slow trickle.

He explained,

Drip, drip, drip. Trauma, trauma, trauma. But all the traumas in my life allowed me to be a really good trauma chaplain. Trauma became my greatest teacher. A lot of people resent their traumas, and I certainly did, but I've learned they are like any of my other scars. My trauma tells people that I have endured something and come out the other side. My places of trauma became places where I could be with people and take them at their worst moments, accept them and accompany them through it. Trauma is kind of like an old-fashioned tape recorder that's always in you. And there's a big red button that says play. And things in life push that button and you can't stop it. I've learned to just let it play its natural course and acknowledge that this is in me. The more I let it play and learn to deal with the emotions that come with it, the less I am controlled by it.

While he spoke to me, James clasped his hands on the table in front of him. I thought of how many times those hands had provided comfort, peace, prayer. He paused, reflecting:

I remember one time I was doing my paperwork after a long night of traumas and I was just burned out. I was burned out and frustrated and questioning God. I had seen so much trauma and so many seriously injured people. I was cursing God with one part of me before I even realized another part of me was saying the Lord's Prayer. That is my life. God is eternally renewing me and giving me hope when I think I am at the end. And I don't keep that hope to myself—I share it. And when I share, it helps heal my trauma and the trauma of those around me.

James reaffirmed to me that even in moments when someone has already died, when medically they need nothing from me, I should still try to bring peace to their body. One morning, I was at the firehouse preparing for rescue training when one of the chiefs walked through the kitchen and nonchalantly stated, "There's a car by the prison with a dead body inside. We have to go get it out."

I looked at the car when we arrived on the scene—it sat buried in the trees on the side of the road. Looking at it from the front, I could see the top of the patient's forehead and some curly, strawberry blond hair. We trekked back through the trees and gathered around the car, readying our rubber gloves, expecting to be the muscle that moved his body into the body bag and then into the waiting ambulance. Instead, I heard my name called.

"Is Ali here?"

I walked to the front of the group.

"'Sup, fellas?"

It was the medic/EMT team I worked with most frequently on the ambulance. They offered a cheery "good morning" before getting down to business.

"So he's laid out across the front of the car and we can't get his hips over the center console. Would you be so kind . . . ?"

They motioned inside, and as if they were inviting me to enter a fancy car, bowed with a "m' lady." The group chuckled. I climbed into the back seat, having to muscle it open, as it had crumpled from impact. Pushing aside the deployed side curtain airbag, I slipped on the chicken wings and French fries that had spilled out of a take-out box. Inside was a quiet grave. I looked at the driver and saw no injuries aside from a red mark on his forehead.

"I think he snapped his neck and that was it," the medic offered, sticking his head through the driver's-side window. "That's what it looks like," I said, hooking my fingers through the driver's belt loops before I called out the one-two-three to those standing outside. We carefully zipped him up into the body bag and then placed him in the ambulance, sending him on to his next destination.

Your time in the tunnel changes you. It's where you learn just how resilient you are and it's where you learn who can keep you company on your journey. Who can shine a flashlight ahead of you to help you see? Who has already found their way out of their tunnel and can remind you to keep persevering? Sometimes you go down a route and find a dead end. You have to turn around and backtrack, feeling like you've not gotten any closer to the sunlight. But that route needed to be explored. The path needed to be walked for you to see that it wasn't the way out, and it's getting you one step closer to the exit.

Every single struggle, no matter the intensity or duration, is a tunnel and not a cave. There is always, *always* a way through. I know that because I know that the version of you who is reading this has the ability to make the necessary choices to find your way through. You're strong enough to find it, resilient enough to keep moving, and brave enough to tackle what you find on your way out.

Maybe you feel like you've been walking in circles, banging your head against the wall, or have been stuck in the dark for a while. Maybe you feel completely controlled by this "inner experience" and aren't sure how to find a new direction. In a *Harvard Business Review* article entitled "Emotional Agility," authors Susan David and Christina Congleton wrote about "getting unhooked." We can do that—breaking that cycle of feeling like we're walking in mental circles—by following the four principles they name: "Recognize your patterns, label your thoughts and emotions, accept them, and act on your values."

REFLECTION AND ACTION

Truth #3 for Overcoming:
Your Struggle Is a Tunnel, Not a Cave

Name one reason you are motivated to keep working to find the light at the end of the tunnel. How can you practice the four principles to help you change direction? If you were to recognize your patterns, what sort of cycle would they follow? What labels could you assign to your thoughts and emotions? How can you practice acceptance instead of judgment? And what are your values? How can your actions reflect them?

4

YOUR LIFE IS YOUR RESPONSIBILITY

And I still believe, though there's cracks you'll see.
When I'm on my knees I still believe.
And when I've hit the ground, neither lost nor found, if
you believe in me, I still believe.
                                        —*Mumford & Sons*

Without what happened next, would I have fallen off the tightrope I was balanced on? Would the trauma bomb that was *tick, tick, ticking* inside my brain have found a different spark eventually? Would the symptoms have festered for even longer and been worse when I was no longer able to bury them away? I don't know. All I know is this: this fire department, the one that I thought would be the place of my redemption, had a change in leadership that resulted in varying beliefs about women's roles in their station becoming much more present. I noticed this instantly and started to protect myself in conscious and subconscious ways. This new leadership then rehired a man who, years before as a volunteer, I'd been told, had been expelled due to his horrendous treatment of women firefighters. To this day, I believe he was the worst of them—a deep-in-his-bones misogynist. His hatred for women was clear in every conversation and every interaction. Misogyny was the foundation he stood on, the religion he worshipped. He was the embodiment of the patriarchy, the confluence of the cage and all of its expectations.

I wasn't new at this station and hoped that the positive ways I'd proven myself and contributed to the environment meant that his behavior wouldn't go unchallenged. It broke my heart into pieces to watch what happened, and I still feel sadness for it. I could sense a change in conversation with those I'd previously had a good working relationship and friendship with. I watched people step away from a whispered conversation with him and never look me in the eye again. They simply stopped acknowledging me when I spoke. Slowly but surely, I watched many of the firefighters there turn into one of two types of men: they either cowered around him or matched his behavior in order to be seen as his equal. Initially unsure of which side of the fault line to stand on, many chose to side with him, while others just pretended the line wasn't there at all. This man formalized the casual sexism that already existed there and made it mandatory.

I remember one specific time this man called me a feminist. It's burned into my brain and sits there, just as powerful, next to the memory of the first time I put on fire gear. I don't remember what led to us standing toe-to-toe on that day, but I remember how his lip quivered in disgust as he stood a few inches away from my face. He said—and others implied—that "my feminism" was a deep detraction from my character and was a poison I was spreading, a filthy disease I had brought on myself and was attempting to give to everyone else. I was meant to be deeply ashamed of identifying with the word and the belief behind it.

I never walked around talking about social justice. I just kept showing up, doing my job, refusing to bend. Ultimately, I was a woman who would not bow to him, and this was my ultimate sin. I went to the leadership, and before I even got two words out, I was told I needed to think about what it was about me that made me "so difficult to work with." This lack of action or acknowledgment once again showed me that what was happening to me didn't matter, and therefore, I must not matter. All I saw were men who were getting away with their actions because they lived in a system that would protect them over me at all costs. This, the harmful actions and the lack of response, all of it happening *again*, pushed me off the tightrope I'd been balancing on, and

I landed directly onto that bomb of unprocessed trauma that had been sitting in my brain.

Over the next few months, I became overwhelmed by the experiences from my first firehouse, the out-of-state one where the sexual assault occurred (as I had never properly dealt with them), and this new one. They were like a burdensome winter coat that I had never taken off, and it had been on so long that I couldn't remember how to remove it. Memories I'd forgotten about from my first firehouse came back into my mind as if I wasn't in control of them. Flashbacks. I remembered the time someone called my name and I turned around, only to run right into a firefighter's outstretched hands that then "accidentally" grazed my breasts. On another night, as I questioned why people were refusing to ride the trucks with me, the fire chief turned around, unclipped the pager from his belt, and threw it against the far wall of the bay. I instinctively ducked as it hit the space directly above my locker. It crashed through the drywall and lodged itself next to a stud. The next morning, I went down to the firehouse and was astonished to find the hole covered by new drywall and shiny, fresh paint. It was clean and spotless, as if nothing had ever happened. I brought it up to someone who had been standing next to me as the pager was thrown, and he looked at me as if I were speaking a different language. His eyes squinted down at me—"What the hell are you talking about?"

A call came in and I went to the firehouse, still feeling so called to respond to people's emergencies but unable to see that remaining in that abusive environment was just hurting me further. It was never the job that was the problem but the people I did the job with. As I walked into the station, I said a prayer that I would be safe. While there, the man called me into the radio room as another officer walked behind us as a "witness." *A witness for him or for me?* I remember thinking. As we sat down, he immediately started yelling, accusing me of "disrespecting" him a few days earlier. I had no memory of our supposed interaction, and I racked my brain trying to remember, wondering what exactly he wanted me to apologize for. He took my silence as rebellion and stood up, his body looming over mine.

I was aware enough of my own body to literally feel the hairs on the back of my neck stand up. My heart started beating wildly. My body flooded with adrenaline and my hands started to shake. At my continued silence, as I tried to remember what the hell he was talking about, he slammed his fists down on the desk where I sat, knocking over a mug of pens and highlighters. I watched them fall and bounce almost in slow motion. The other firefighter in the room didn't move or speak. I laid my hands flat on the desk as he stood over me, willing myself to stay present and ready to protect myself. I felt that he could hurt me, really truly hurt me, and no one would stop him. When there was a pause in his screaming, I stood up and wordlessly moved past him to leave. As I pushed the door open, I cut my thumb on a rough metal piece on the door handle. I looked down at the blood and felt nothing. I had left myself.

I drove the few blocks to the house I was living in with my sibling, Julia, and my brother-in-law. I sat in my car in the driveway, heaving with white-hot anger, trying to control a body that did not feel like mine, unable to stand up or take in a full breath. I was capsized. I felt thrown away, so stuck in this cycle that I didn't understand how to break. I looked up to see Julia hurrying toward me with a face full of concern. I managed to get a few words out before my body released the years of stress and pain that had been building up. The grief demanded to be felt, and in that moment, it was more than my body could hold. Kneeling next to me at my open car door, Julia held my hand. I rested my head on the steering wheel, and between full-body sobs, I whispered to myself, "You're OK, you're OK, you're OK."

Once inside, I stripped out of my clothes and sat like a zombie on the floor of the shower for almost an hour. Sitting there, I realized why I couldn't remember doing what this man had accused me of. I was on the complete other side of the station, preparing to hop on a fire truck, when this supposed transgression occurred. We had not interacted at all, so there was no opportunity for me to "disobey him." What he said had happened simply hadn't, but I knew that the truth didn't matter anymore.

He knew that people would believe his word over mine. He'd been laying the groundwork for some time.

I was desperate for time away, so Forrest and I took a weekend to go to his hometown. As we drove away, I could feel myself breathing easier. He held my hand as I stared out the window of his truck, trying so hard to find the pieces of myself that kept fading away. I took in the surroundings as we drove in silence. Next to us, the river had gone cold. Squares of ice floated like giant white lily pads. Dark, leafless trees stood like skeleton hands whose spindly fingers reached upward. The swollen sky promised snow. On the other side of us loomed the chain of mountains that we followed around the valley. Clusters of icicles hung overhead, stories high. It was as if the mountain had been crying and, in a frozen moment, forgot. The forest seemed to stretch on infinitely, as if one could walk across the blinding white forever and never find the end.

Mentally, I was like a wilting flower, curling in on itself in the absence of light. I started to experience what I later learned were panic attacks. I showed no outward anxiety or emotion; it was just the opposite. I would become completely detached and disconnected, as if my brain had reached its capacity for trauma and would just shut down. I would sit on the floor of my bedroom for unknown amounts of time, my mind lost to experiences that happened in the four walls of the firehouse, not feeling safe enough to even go outside.

I was sick to my stomach often during those long months. Constant stress and anxiety made nausea ever-present, and I would often fall asleep next to the toilet in case I threw up. I'd wake up to Forrest standing over me. He'd help me up, pulling a sweatshirt down over my head to stop my shivering. Hives erupted across my skin regularly, as the stress, pain, and trauma were no longer contained to just my mind. The bucket of cumulative stress and trauma I'd been carrying had imploded.

I have had a challenging relationship with my body since joining the fire service. As a young girl, society told me that being skinny was the ultimate "good" thing, an end goal. My thin legs and arms were supposed to make me feel fulfilled and confident. But then firefighting told me that the same small frame was a handicap that I could never get out from under. I looked at broad-shouldered, muscular girls with the same admiration and longing that others look at ultraskinny models. Why were they born with the body I so badly needed? Later, I didn't know how to make that body feel like mine. My brain and body existed as disparate entities, and I wasn't yet able to honor my body for all it had withstood. My body and I had become so distant as I disassociated away from the complicated trauma it held. Taking care of myself didn't feel like a priority anymore, and that manifested through my relationship with food. I felt hollow and empty, but my constant hypervigilance replaced normal hunger with anxious nausea. I wanted to wither away to nothing, and controlling what I ate made me feel some power over the body I had great hatred for.

When I speak these days, I break it down in this way. The trauma I'd experienced taught me three things, and this was how my brain had organized into disorder:

1. The world was not a safe place.
2. People could not be trusted.
3. Everything that happened was my fault.

I didn't know that adverse life experiences could affect our mental health to this degree, so I was walking around thinking I had truly lost my mind. I could not fathom how other people walked around in their lives without feeling like something life-ruining was just around the corner. That felt impossible to me, otherworldly. I continued to devour other people's stories of triumph and felt envious when the "bad guy" was universally agreed on. The "bad guy" could be cancer, mother nature, a freak accident. But in the story I was living, if you asked the people in it with me, I was the bad guy—the answer was *me*.

I didn't see how someone could walk around holding so many unanswered questions. They played on a loop in my mind:

Why did this happen to you?

Why did you ever walk into a firehouse to begin with?

Why did you try again?

What did you expect?

Why did you fail again?

Why do you always fail?

I felt like I lived in a parallel universe where my pain was invisible and insignificant to almost everyone else. I lived in a world where all I saw was a complete lack of consequence, lack of visibility, lack of witness, lack of help. I was living on the razor's edge of pain, bleeding from trauma both old and new. Even the slightest pressure on my throat became all I could focus on until I could rid myself of that feeling. Any sort of necklace, the collar of any shirt, a scarf, a seat belt, my bed covers. My body was remembering that night at the firehouse all those years ago. I let Forrest and Hannah in to some degree, and my family too, but other than that, I had isolated myself. Through a text, I told Forrest that I was making myself an island. He responded, "Then I'm a patrol boat." Still, isolation was my biggest negative coping skill.

Negative coping skills are things we do to decrease our stress or numb pain that only help us in the short term. Imagine you're standing at the entrance to a bridge, and on the other side of the valley is your whole future.

Making sure we get enough rest, eating food that fuels our bodies instead of depleting them, and relying on support systems are examples of things that help us stay on the path and are healthy ways of coping. Relying on a negative coping skill over time like drinking alcohol to fall asleep is like blowing that bridge up. You can still get to the other side; it's just going to take longer, and the journey will be a lot harder on you and everyone around you.

When you get a cut, the body immediately begins the healing process without your knowledge or effort. Your blood vessels contract and platelets release proteins that mix together to coagulate and clot your blood. White blood cells rush to the area to attack any bacteria that entered your body, and your skin cells begin to reproduce to close up the wound. When you experience trauma, your body knows to do the same thing. Interrupting that process by using negative coping skills is going to increase the time you stay wounded. They are a barrier to healing.

We use negative coping skills because they work . . . but only for a while. They give us temporary relief from the pain, a momentary breath without holding the weight. But then that negative coping skill becomes just another thing we have to overcome. If it was possible to outwill trauma, to outachieve it, to ignore it into oblivion, that's what this book would have been about. You are not going to be the first person to discover that simply ignoring your trauma will allow you to live the kind of life you want—it just doesn't work like that. Trust me.

At that point, with what was available to me, the only way I could see to stop the pain was to shut off my emotions and tourniquet them like a dying limb. It turns out that you can't really pick and choose what emotions you let in. Turning off the tap to some numbs them all. But things weren't bad every single second. I could smile in pictures or give life advice to my friends when they asked. I could share the parts of my story I'd found meaning in. My entire life wasn't out of control; I was still functioning. To the people who knew me during that time who are reading this, I understand that you might feel surprised at the intensity of what I was dealing with. It just goes to show how good we are at hiding the pain we are in. I lived with Hannah during a lot of this time, but even she didn't know all of what was going on behind my bedroom door. It proves that we truly don't know what someone is dealing with. A smiling face, a curated Instagram, a wall full of framed achievements, or a big bank account does not mean anything in terms of what one is dealing with.

A shadow was cast over every single second, a fear that never went away. I was preoccupied with how to be believed, with how to make sure I wasn't ever alone with any man I didn't know, with how to avoid anyone who was drinking or drunk. This was the "I didn't think it was bad enough" portion of my life, the same sentiment I've heard from so many others.

At the time, I felt the need to have an immediate exit behind me at all times and to wear pants with an uncomfortably tight belt because that would make it harder for someone to rip them off, giving me more time to fight. I thought the only logical response was to wall myself off from anyone and anything that posed a threat. Then those habits began to make sense in the outside world, not just in the firehouse.

People ask what made me finally want to go get help, and there was no crisis moment, no sudden breaking point. The simple truth was that I just got sick of this version of myself. I got sick of the suffocating darkness. I didn't want to wait for it to get worse. One night as I was sitting on the floor of my room, awake as usual since sleeping brought nightmares, I thought of a kind woman named Jill who lived kitty-corner to my parents. All I knew about her was that she was a counselor. I didn't know what kind or if she'd want to talk with me, but I texted her the three most courageous words I've ever said to anyone: "I need help."

The next day, I found myself walking to Jill's office, talking myself out of it and turning around, wanting to return to the comfort of my isolated island more than a few times. The pain felt easier to contain if I kept it to myself. But that belief was slowly killing me, and I knew it. I had to take responsibility for what the rest of my life was going to look like. I made it to Jill's office and sat in front of her in a comfortable chair when I took what felt like the biggest risk of my life.

I told her everything, using whatever words I had at the time. She did not judge, she did not blame, she was not shocked—she just listened. When I felt finished, she told me that, given what I had gone through, being as affected as I was "made sense." When I saw that she wasn't going to dismiss me, I relaxed.

I know how lucky I am to have clicked with the first therapist I tried. I hope that if I hadn't found her initially, I would have kept trying until I found someone who was the right fit for me. If you've had a negative or just ineffective therapy experience but think you could really benefit from talking to a therapist, keeping trying until you find your Jill.

After we talked for a while, Jill pulled out a thick book that looked like a dictionary. She started reading to me some symptoms that correlated with a disorder. With every symptom she offered, I nodded, as I'd been feeling them all. She closed the book and looked at me, waiting for me to understand that I had something called post-traumatic stress disorder (PTSD). She told me that I had an injury to the part of my brain that dealt with stress and fear and that my experiences in firehouses hurt me in a real and literal way. It was like they took a baseball bat to my leg and broke it, she said. She told me that the depths I was in at that moment didn't have to be where I lived forever.

Many of us fear going to therapy because we don't want a label; we don't want someone to tell us we "have something." But when Jill told me about post-traumatic stress disorder, she freed me from thinking I had brought this upon myself or made it up. Those four words gave me a name and a cause and a reason. They were the validation and visibility I craved. PTSD gave the monster in my head a name. It made the monster not my fault and its existence not my choice. Armed with the knowledge of what my symptoms were called, I wanted to know who I could be without them.

Cumulative stress or long-lasting trauma can be like collecting drops in a bucket that eventually overflows or adding more five-pound weights to our bodies until we eventually collapse. For me, it was like being pulled farther and farther out into the ocean. For a while in the beginning, my feet were firm on the ground, and I could stand up to the waves that came. But every time the waves receded, they drew me farther away from the shore. I treaded water for years. There were times when I could float on my back, staring up at the sky, hoping that the next wave that came would take me back to safety. But that never happened. Every harmful action drew me farther out, but silence from the "good guys" is what wore me down to the point where I didn't want to swim anymore. Storms came in the form of blame, excuses, the "boys will be boys" of it all, the ever-present systemic sexism, the feeling of invisibility, the lack of action, the shame.

I was angry at myself for not being able to stay afloat longer. I was furious that what had continued to happen to me wasn't enough to make anyone else think or act differently. So it felt easier to stop fighting. Expending all that energy didn't seem to be helping me. So I sank. I found a place on the bottom of the ocean where I could make myself small and silent. Waves rolled overhead, but I couldn't feel them anymore. I anchored my love for firefighting like a boulder to my chest, refusing to let it go. My knuckles were white, fingertips bleeding. And yet I felt comforted in my quiet cocoon. There was no looking toward the future, no dreaming, only the next moment. I sat as still as a stone, hibernating. But I wasn't doing nothing. I went where I had to go to make myself safe, to rest, and to become someone who was prepared to fight for her own life.

Thinking of reaching out to Jill was like me opening my eyes and looking up to see that there was light up above me. And I thought that there was a tiny possibility that if I got to that light, to help, I could get back to the shore. I didn't know if Jill would or could help, or if anyone would. I didn't know what was wrong with me or if whatever it was could be fixed. But I knew that I was tired of being the Sunken Girl. And while inside my quiet cocoon, I'd had time to remember how strong my legs were, and they'd gotten their needed rest. I was ready to swim again. I needed to drop the boulder, be prepared to leave firefighting behind, take the chance that my time with it had passed, and be willing to step out of the water as someone new.

Walking to Jill's office for the first time was me kicking my legs and swimming to the light. Only I could decide that I was ready to tell the stories, to risk telling the truth, to simply try something other than what I'd been doing. Talking to Jill didn't get me out of the water right away. But it brought my head above the surface, to the light, to a place where I could breathe. She understood why I'd been sunk, told me that swimming back was going to be exhausting but that I wouldn't be by myself, and pointed me in the direction of the shore.

My dad swam next to me, telling me that I "always have more in the tank," that I always have enough energy to keep going. My mom was there too, telling me that I am stronger than I could ever imagine and that I was not alone. Julia was there, telling me to keep my head up. Hannah was there too, telling me that I was brave and saying prayers with me. Forrest held me up when I was tired, never letting go. At times, they swam next to me, just keeping me company. Other times, they swam ahead, showing me the way. They all helped me take my first steps in the sand.

It's easy to look back at our sunken selves and judge them. We think that we could have gotten out of the water sooner. We shouldn't have gone in so deep. We should have decided to kick our legs long before we did. But I have no regrets for the ways I chose to make myself safe, and I hope you don't either. We used the tools and life experiences that were available to us at the time. Have grace for the version of yourself who did what they needed to do to be safe. There is a space in my heart for the Sunken Girl. When I think of her, I thank her for resting when she had to and for sticking around to make this version of me so damn resilient.

I can stand on the shore and look out at the vast expanse now, hold the entirety of this story in me and connect with the Sunken Girl without becoming her. I know that if a memory ever comes up and hurts, as trauma does, if I ever find myself up to my shins in the water again, I can turn around and walk right back out. I can grasp any number of hands that are outstretched toward me.

Even those closest to you cannot be there every moment, when the darkness fits like a heavy winter coat or when the jagged edge of a memory threatens to split you open at your seams. I knew those men were responsible for my hurt, but I had also thought that made them responsible for my overcoming of it. Finally realizing they had nothing to do with the rest of my life is what helped me begin. The overcoming doesn't feel any different in the beginning. You're not magically better. The difference is that you know you have another option than just being sunk; you know what the sunlight feels like. So take whatever cards you were dealt, choose your rest, then find your legs, and fucking swim.

Since stepping into the counseling community myself, I've noticed a tendency to overpathologize trauma. There is an inclination to draw linear lines between an experience and its anticipated trigger, to expect that people who have felt trauma will hold it or identify with it in the same way, to forget that there is a *person* in addition to their symptoms. The way shame blocks one's ability to comfort the younger versions of ourselves that were hurt is discounted and dismissed. I've seen non-trauma-informed therapists take an approach that is too intellectual. They list positive coping skills, offer the definition of resilience, and send people on their way. But trauma is *felt*. It is lived in all our relationships, especially the relationship we have with ourselves.

Trauma is stored in little pockets of our brains, written into our cells, carried in our blood. We can only shed it the same way we got it—through experience. We must look at overcoming trauma through a holistic lens, by supporting people through new positive experiences that help rewrite the parts of their brains that learned fear, through movement to release the stored stress our bodies hold, through acknowledging losses, and by supporting the meaning-making process. And we must walk with survivors on their path to assure them above all else that they are worthy of receiving the help they need to hold the weight and that someday it will not feel so heavy.

Recently, I met with Jill again to revisit our work together. Our winter boots crunched on the gravel as we walked in circles around a newly built baseball field in my hometown. I asked her to recount what she remembered about the first time we'd started working together all those years earlier. She was exactly as I'd remembered: warm and affirming.

As we walked, Jill told me, "I remember that your experiences were very protected, especially the sexual assault. You held so much shame and blame around everything. So much of our work in the beginning was around 'Was this as bad as I feel it was and how much of it was my fault?'"

I told her that I remembered her pulling out what I now know was the DSM (*Diagnostic and Statistical Manual of Mental Disorders*) and reading the symptoms and definition of PTSD to me. She nodded, smiling:

> You know, I never do that. I never just pull out the DSM and start to read, but I sensed that it's what you needed. I felt that you could look at PTSD objectively, almost medically, and see its legitimacy that way. You needed the proof, and you needed to walk yourself to the answer. I

remember reading you the symptoms and watching you nod at every single one. I told you that you only needed so many to warrant the diagnosis and, Ali, I remember the moment when it came over you. I remember when you finally and fully realized what I had been telling you: that you had something called post-traumatic stress disorder, that it was real, and that it was not your fault. You had a tendency to want to skip the hurt and go right to the healing. That had been your protection for so long—avoiding the hurt—but avoiding it wasn't going to heal it.

I told her about the time I'd been sharing my story onstage when I noticed a woman sitting in front of me in the audience start to cry. I almost always notice this and make it a point to find that person afterward if they don't find me first. When she found me, she told me that her trauma had recently been demanding to be dealt with and that she'd found the name and number of a therapist but hadn't yet reached out to her. She'd started crying because that therapist was also named Jill, and she took it as her sign to reach out and take responsibility for the rest of her life. I told Jill about the countless people who come up to me and tell me that they're willing to try to find their own Jill. I mentioned that so many people working in the emergency services were led to believe that "We don't talk about it" was the only way, but through my story, they are learning that it is never too late to begin the work.

After beginning my work with Jill, as I was finding my footing on the shore, my best friend, Hannah, needed some help finding words for a trauma that had happened to her. Her experiences didn't fit neatly into a box, but she knew they'd deeply hurt her. I took Hannah to the place where I knew there would be answers, where there would be people willing to give her the words she needed. I walked with her, swam beside her, to the local Women's Resource Center, where she met counselors who validated her. I thought that I'd like to help survivors in that same way someday. I felt drawn to advocacy and wanted to find a way to help people find their resilience the way Jill had helped me find mine. I wanted to start in the place where I'd been so hurt, and this led me to work with sexual assault survivors.

Author Diane Coutu defines resilience as "the skill and capacity to be robust under conditions of enormous stress and change." Being resilient is a process we have to actively participate in and take responsibility for. Just like any other muscle in our bodies or any other skill we've learned, we become more resilient through practice. No one else can do it for us. We can have company along the way and someone to guide us, but we have to decide that our lives are our responsibility and that we are willing to put in the work to get to where we want to be. Coutu also discusses what her research showed her about resilient people: "Resilient people, they posit, possess three characteristics: a staunch acceptance of reality; a deep belief, often buttressed by strongly held values, that life is meaningful; and an uncanny ability to improvise."

Learned helplessness can be unlearned, and resilience can take its place. We can challenge it by asking ourselves, "What is the most empowering decision available to me right now?" and taking one small step toward that. One kick in the water. That can look like asking for help until we actually get it. You can also beat learned helplessness by telling someone you trust about what you are experiencing or believing that you are strong enough to leave a situation that is no longer serving you. Asking for help and admitting that you're not fine could be the hardest conversation you ever have. But being brave for those few moments, having those moments of courage, can be what sets your life on a whole new course.

REFLECTION AND ACTION

Truth #4 for Overcoming:
Your Life Is Your Responsibility

What would you do, where would you go, and what conversations are you waiting to have until you're "better"? What if you did those things today? Can you find your legs and kick, even just a little? How can you increase your ability to be resilient based on the three qualities we learned? Name the changes you are waiting to make and then list steps you can take today to get there.

5

THERE IS NO ONE RIGHT WAY TO BE A SURVIVOR

We are not justifying it. We are redeeming it.
—*William Paul Young,* The Shack

With my feet firmly on the shore again, I decided to become a volunteer domestic violence and sexual assault counselor and advocate for the same women's resource center I'd taken Hannah to. Twice a week, I walked to the unassuming building that housed the staff's offices but also served as housing for women and children escaping their abusers. I sat in the classroom with other counselors-in-training as we learned about trauma and its aftershocks.

I was living my story every day, not shying away from the conversations readers of *Where Hope Lives* wanted to have with me. I never knew who was going to find that story and in what ways it would impact them.

Unbeknownst to me, a firefighter from my firehouse purchased a copy of *Where Hope Lives* and gave it to a local EMT. After she read it, he told her, "This is your fire company." This girl was currently a firefighter in the place where I'd started. She reached out to me on social media and asked to meet with me, which we did at a local coffee shop. As I was writing this second book, many years after first meeting with her, I asked if she'd be willing to revisit that time in her life. We reconnected one night over Zoom.

She told me that when she first joined the firehouse, they reviewed with her a binder of rules, including a big section on sexual harassment. She remembers thinking that I didn't have that, so that was a new, potentially positive change. But that seems to be as far as the changes went. Another woman firefighter volunteered at the station as well, and she remembers watching the male firefighters physically push her to the ground and then pretend to pee on her. She shook her head as she told me this, shrugging her shoulders in disbelief. I thought of my younger self standing there as she had, in disbelief at what I was seeing. She told me about another night when she stood in the group as others prepared to try on new fire gear. In front of everyone, the firefighter who was in charge beckoned at her to "come." As she started to move toward him, he exclaimed, "Ha! Made you come with two fingers."

At this, I exhaled slowly. We stared at each other through our computer screens, two brown-haired, brown-eyed girls from the same town who experienced some of the same treatment from the same men within the same four walls. I take major issue when people attempt to excuse this behavior or lessen it by saying, "These men don't know any better." That's an absolute lie and a complete abdication of responsibility. They don't say these things to their child's teacher during a parent-teacher conference. They don't say them to the person ringing up their groceries. They say them when and where they know they can, when those comments will be met with laughter or silence.

She asked a guy friend from school to join the fire company, and she would only go if he was there too. She told me that the training was really fun initially, but after a while, it was "too painful to be there," so she decided to leave. I asked her if she thought she'd ever join another fire company, and she shook her head: "No. They burned the image I have of firefighters pretty much forever."

We took different paths on our way out of that environment, and our paths in and out of the emergency services have continued to diverge, but both are completely valid. Your reaction to an experience doesn't have to look like anyone else's, even if you experienced something really similar to someone else. Return to the environment if it deserves you, or leave it for good. Use your voice to tell your story publicly or tell it to a trusted chosen few. There is no one right way.

I had never wanted to be onstage during shows in high school, preferring to work behind the scenes. Now speaking in front of packed auditoriums while standing among set pieces was my job. I would get up at 3:00 a.m., spend hours in the car, speak at a school at 8:00 a.m., and then drive home, exhausted but exhilarated. I was living my purpose. One week I spoke to four thousand students at twelve separate speaking engagements.

Once, after speaking at a middle school, I noticed a girl with light-blonde hair standing at the end of a long line of students who were waiting to talk with me. Something about her caught my eye. When it was her turn to speak, she stepped forward and started to talk to me in a whisper. Immediately, I leaned in and tried to file away every piece of information, as I knew I would have to repeat it. She spoke of years of horrific sexual abuse at the hands of her mother, of not feeling like she'd be believed by her father, and so she'd never told anyone. She ducked her head toward my shoulder, a tear shining down her pale cheek. I grasped her forearms and spoke quietly but with firm intention: "I am going to tell someone, OK? I'm going to tell someone. You're not alone with this anymore."

She looked up at me silently, her eyes full of hope.

I told her teacher, who'd been waiting nearby, and together we went and told the principal, all of us mandated reporters. A few hours later, I was at home in my room on the phone with Childline, reporting her abuse. I received an email later that evening: "Hi Ali. I don't know if you remember me but we talked today after your presentation at my school. I told you what was happening to me. You told me you would tell someone and you did. People came to my house a little bit ago. My dad knows now and he believes me. I don't know what I would have done if you didn't come to my school today. You are the only person who has ever given me a voice. Thank you."

A friend's mom asked me to speak about *Where Hope Lives* at her book club. I drove four hours to speak to the handful of book club members at a Panera. Another woman, Linda, decided my book would be perfect for her group of high schoolers, many of whom had experienced adversity, most of whom had never finished a book before. I visited her class once and then returned multiple times over a few semesters. I listened to her students and heard their stories, their struggles, their pain, their hope, their resilience. I listened, stunned and honored, at what *Where Hope Lives* was teaching them about forgiveness and the ability to choose their own paths. Linda and I decided to develop a lesson plan around *Where Hope Lives* that would last them an entire year. We wrote personal mission statements and letters of forgiveness to ourselves or others. On my last visit, they lined up in front of me and shook my hand one by one. They thanked me for helping them realize who they were, what they stood for, what they wanted for their lives, and how to be brave. Linda started to cry. "You're changing their lives," she whispered to me. They were stepping into their After.

After another speaking engagement, I watched a group of shy middle schoolers coax their friend up to me. I had talked with about a dozen students that day, offering encouragement and validity and talking about additional resources for them. I'd been watching this group slowly shuffle up to me, as the three girls persuaded their male friend ahead of them. They waited until everyone except me and a guidance counselor in the back of the room had left the auditorium. This middle schooler stood in front of me. I noticed all three of his friends were crying, but his eyes were clear. I looked down at him, opening up my heart to hear another story of pain, and hoping the right words of comfort would come. I waited, not pressuring him. His cheeks were flushed, but he spoke flatly: "I was going to kill myself when I got home from school today. I've tried twice before and I know how to not mess it up this time. After hearing what you had to say about better days and not giving up . . . I thought maybe there could be better days for me too."

The stage lights had been turned off, so as he spoke, he was cast in a shadow. He fiddled with the pocket of his dirty hoodie. He looked so young, too little to be in this much pain. I put my hands on his shoulders, pulled him close to me, and looked right into his eyes: "I promise you there are. I promise."

I motioned to the guidance counselor to come to us. His face started to melt into tears as I hugged him tightly.

I was almost late for the next talk. Someone handed me a microphone as I walked in the door to the high school gym, and I turned to see a wall of students sitting on the tiered bleachers. More than nine hundred students and me. I dropped my bag and talked for an hour about bravery and standing up, about the purpose of telling your story and being true to yourself. We talked about boundaries and not changing just because other people are saying that you have to. I stood on that floor long after the microphone left my hand, hearing stories and offering support, validation, and hope.

After graduating from the domestic violence and sexual assault counselor/advocate class, I took a part-time job working nights and weekends at the domestic violence shelter. The residents there were fleeing potentially lethal abuse. I'd read through the new residents' files to learn about what brought them to us. Their files held basic information, recent injuries, hospital visits, information about their children, any contact with police, concerns about their abusers coming to our building, and the make and model of their abusers' vehicles. I'd peer out at the parking lot before turning off the lights at night to make sure I didn't see any of those vehicles.

Occasionally, a resident would wander into our office or a toddler would find their way into the hallway that separated the staff and residential spaces. These women told me their stories and I did my best to simply bear witness and offer words of support and hope. They told me of lives in foster care, of being neglected since birth, of being injected with heroin by a parent at the age of eight, of being raped by their father every year on their birthday.

One night while on call in the middle of a snowstorm, I was asked to respond to the hospital to be an advocate for a survivor of sexual assault who'd just arrived. I clutched the wheel of my Honda Civic and peered ahead of me through the swirling snow. Kicking snow off my shoes, I walked into the emergency department as the survivor was telling the forensic nurse that multiple men at a fraternity party had just taken turns raping her on a bed as she went in and out of consciousness.

"I was facedown the whole time, so I don't know what anyone looked like."

I introduced myself and told her what my role was there. As I spoke, I looked at the clothes she was wearing, the ones she put back on as she stepped into her After. I started talking to her about all the options that were available to her, like a full rape kit and medicine to prevent pregnancy, HIV, and STIs. She had the option to make a report to the police, but she did not have to.

"I just want this to be over. I want to go home."

Her four friends sat wide-eyed next to her, arms crossed against the chill of the room, unsure of what to do.

"Listen," I said quietly. "I know you don't want to be here anymore, I know. I know you just want to start putting this behind you. But this is not something that is going to go away when you leave this hospital. It's going to be with you every day for a while. You didn't get to choose that this happened to you, but you can choose what you do now, in this moment. And no matter what you choose to do, we'll support you."

There is so much power in reaffirming someone's simple ability to make choices about what happens to their own body, especially after that choice has been taken away.

In every situation, it is the survivor who is responsible for bearing the damage, consequences, and truth of their abuser's actions. We are required to possess the poise and eloquence to be believable if we do decide to speak but not so strong that we are seen as intimidating or aggressive. I invite you to challenge your understanding of what sexual assault is.

Some truths: Sexual assault is most often perpetuated by a person known to the survivor, not a complete stranger, as is often portrayed. Husbands can rape wives. Boyfriends can rape girlfriends. Same-sex couples can perpetrate sexual assault against each other. Non-penetrative sexual assault is still very much an assault. If someone is intoxicated, they legally cannot give consent, so if you assume silence or even unconsciousness equals consent, you are incorrect.

Survivors are still telling the truth if they choose to report their assault years or even decades later. Going to the police immediately after an assault does not mean they will (1) take the survivor seriously, (2) investigate fully, or (3) hold anyone accountable. Having a rape kit done also does not mean the perpetrator will be caught. Hundreds of thousands of rape kits are untested in this country (#EndtheBacklog). If a woman doesn't fight back during an assault, it does not mean she wanted it. It means that she was trying to stay alive.

The right question isn't "Why did it take her so long to tell her story?" but "Why does anyone come forward at all?" We know what's waiting for us. It's as predictable as the sun rising—the character assassination, the lies—but we do it simply because the truth has to mean something. And as long as there is someone to tell it, we won't be buried.

As a part of my work with the domestic violence shelter, I spent time answering the crisis hotline. My first priority while on the phone with a client was to ensure that they were safe enough to be on the phone with me.

In response, I'd hear things like "Yeah, he's passed out in the other room" or "I'm locked in the bathroom. He thinks I'm talking to my mom."

They would ask a lot of the same questions in different ways:

Was this rape?
Does this count as abuse?
Will he do it again?
Will he kill me the next time?
What did I do to deserve this?
Will he ever start hurting my children the same
way he hurts me?

Whenever children were mentioned, I had to glean additional information to potentially make a Childline report on their behalf. If there was immediate, life-threatening danger and the caller wanted me to, I would contact the on-call district magistrate and explain the details of the situation to see if they would grant an emergency protection from abuse, known as an E-PFA. The next step would be to see if there was a bed for the caller and their children at our shelter if they wanted one. If they wanted to stay where they were, we would plan ways they could stay as safe as possible.

The people who work in these organizations are heroes. They choose to sit with the ugliness of the world and hold the pain of others so they don't have to bear it alone. They show up for each and every survivor, working tirelessly to make a difference for them. So often people walk around with their hands over their eyes; they don't want to know the realities of the world around them. But these people learn everything they can about abuse and abusers to increase the chances that they'll be able to say the right thing at the right time to help that person get to safety. Their words and their actions say to survivors, "I see you. What happened to you was never OK, and it was never your fault. You aren't alone with it anymore."

Some of us have the instinct to turn away when we hear of violence, trauma, or oppression. I have been that person. My worldview hadn't yet been cracked wide open by the ugly truths that surround us. I thought it wasn't my business, until it was suddenly very much my business. The women I meet through doing this work and sharing my story are some of the strongest and most resilient human beings I have ever met. We weave together these stories of pain and anger, hoping that there is strength in numbers, hoping that somehow, if we can summon the strength to rip open the wound we worked so hard to seal, we will find similarities in the way we bleed and, despite our different circumstances and backgrounds and voices, we will find a way to take violence and turn it into power, to find a way, some way, any way, to make it so we won't ever have to hear anyone say, "Me too."

My friend Victoria is a mental health educator, author, and survivor of childhood abuse. She explained what overcoming means during a conversation with her mom about intergenerational abuse. Victoria talked about how the developmental trauma she experienced means her brain functions differently than others, and because her mother was abused while Victoria was in the womb, her trauma started prior to her birth. I love how Victoria talked about how overcoming trauma can be a lifelong process but that we need to "give ourselves credit for being the beautiful, extraordinary, courageous, vulnerable human being that we are."

I remember a wordless but powerful interaction I had with a woman during and after one of my keynote addresses. I was speaking in front of a group of six hundred or so firefighters in Phoenix, Arizona. I'd gotten stuck in Dallas the night before as a thunderstorm raged over the airport and would not budge. I'd finally made it to Phoenix and had just an hour or two of sleep before I stepped on stage to keynote. I started to talk about the freedom I learned when I stopped abiding by the expectations that existed for me in firehouses. The freedom that I feel in not staying inside the tiny little box of expectations, the cage that was built for me. I talked briefly about society's expectations of me, and of all women, and how I had to first learn to recognize the cage if I was ever going to break out of it.

As I spoke, I noticed a woman in the audience, sitting next to someone I assumed to be her husband. There was something about the look on her face that kept drawing my attention as I scanned the room while I spoke. When I started talking about freedom from these expectations, I essentially said it right to her, feeling like she was sitting in that room to hear me say those words. Her eyes were wide, fixated on mine. Seeing this exchange, her husband put his large arm across the back of her chair, and as I continued to speak, he wrapped it around her shoulder as if he were protecting her from my words.

After I finished and had talked to a few dozen people one-on-one, I noticed her standing across the hallway looking at me. Her husband was talking to someone else but held her hand firmly, like a handcuff binding her to him. Suddenly, her husband saw me looking at her and marched them away. I wanted to tell her that her story is worth being heard. I wanted to tell her that even if she can't tell it right now, she will never run out of time to do so.

It's easy to be the person who stands on a stage. It's harder to be the person who steps off it, to be the person people tell their secrets to. It takes a lot of energy to be the bearer of otherwise untold stories, to be the person who stands in the space between who someone was before and who they are after they've told their truth. Over time, I have learned how to grow my capacity to hold these stories. While it can be energy-draining, I would not trade it for anything on the earth. It is a sacred space to watch a secret lose its power as it's said out loud. *Tell me. Tell me so you don't have to hold it alone. I'll take it so you can walk away, free.*

We think that if our stories have similarities to other people's, why bother telling it? We think our stories aren't anything special or that every person we know has experienced something they've had to overcome. We think that so much time has passed, certainly no one would care anymore. We should be "over it" by now. I've heard these sentiments easily hundreds of times. The statute of limitations places an expiration date on our ability to seek justice in some cases, but your ability to stand in your survivorship never expires.

There is no right way to do any of this—surviving. Stand on a stage or stand in front of your bathroom mirror. Speak your truth into a microphone or write it onto a piece of paper. Tell it to your trusted people or tell the story of your survival to just yourself. Some find power in standing in their stories and sharing it. I found power in advocacy. Every time I stand on a stage or share my story in any context, I am asserting that I have the power to tell the truth, but your story doesn't need to be applauded for your overcoming to be real. You are no more or less brave if a room full of people knows what you've gone through. You don't need to make a social media post about your overcoming to make it real. The difficult experience you had doesn't have to classify as trauma or abuse for you to be impacted. You don't have to confront or befriend those who made you a survivor in order for your overcoming to be the new solid foundation you stand on. You don't have to embrace those who hurt you for your overcoming to be legitimate. You do not owe your truth or your trauma to anyone. Telling your story to yourself is just as brave.

REFLECTION AND ACTION

Truth #5 for Overcoming:
There Is No One Right Way to Be a Survivor

You are a survivor whether anyone else knows it or not. There is no one you owe your truth to, but our stories demand to be acknowledged. Without carrying the pressure of any "should," what additions would you want to make to the ways you carry your story?

PART II

Just when the caterpillar thought the world was over, it became a butterfly.

—proverb

6

YOUR RELATIONSHIP TO YOUR
STORY WILL CHANGE OVER TIME

*Leave it to me as I find a way to be. Consider me a
satellite forever orbiting.
I knew all the rules but the rules did not know me,
guaranteed.*

—Eddie Vedder

Mine and Forrest's wedding was a day filled with love
and joy. The husband of my beloved trauma therapist
Jill, a pastor, performed our ceremony. The picture of
the four of us is one of my favorites from that whole day.

One week after our wedding, Forrest drove me to the
police station, my wedding pedicure still on my toes. I
sat across from a detective and told him everything
I'd experienced in local firehouses. I told him names,
situations, experiences, and dates. The detective wrote

everything down in an official report. He added *Where Hope Lives* as evidence. It was so strange to think that my story was also serving as proof. My goal wasn't to prosecute or bring charges to anyone, but I wanted to make an official record for my sixteen-year-old self and be a voice for the girl who had been rendered voiceless.

I sat in an interview room and laid out everything I'd written in my journals. I shared what I'd been told when I'd first joined—that some of the firefighters were "violent and dangerous" and that one had "raped a minor" in the kitchen of the station. I'd had naked pictures sent to my phone and porn shoved into my locker—the list of violations went on and on. The detective took notes as I spoke. When I was done, I waited for his response, thinking back to when I sat in the front seat of that police car with his colleague. He told me that the police officer should have had a conversation with each person involved and told them that the harassment, stalking, cyberbullying—all of it—ended right then and there, and if it didn't, then there would be consequences and potential criminal charges. "I'm sorry that this didn't happen when you were going through all of that. It should have."

Justice doesn't always look like punishment or jail time. Sometimes justice looks like being believed, and in that moment, I was.

While packing up the house I lived in before I was married, I reached under my bed and found the small blue collapsible knife I tucked there when I first moved in. My fingers curled around the well-worn handle and remembered all the times I carried it in firehouses like my life depended on it. I stood in my bedroom and cried, a cleansing, feeling a sense of all the struggles those walls had held. I finally felt on the edge of a new chapter. I've often heard that "you cannot heal in the same environment that hurt you," and I really believe this is true. There was only so much I could do while still waiting to see these faces around town.

Forrest and I drove into Philadelphia in the middle of a heat wave, two weeks to the day after we were married. As Forrest parked the massive U-Haul in front of our new townhouse, I felt like I'd finally crossed the finish line of the marathon I'd been running. I had gotten away.

As time passed in this new town, it was as if someone had wrapped a blanket around my memories. Like running your thumb across the blade of a butter knife, I could get close to them and not be cut. I had been living with chronic mental pain every day for over a decade. It had become a part of me—that mental ache, that absence of safety, the void of that younger version of myself who I was still searching for. But in my new house, I would go to bed each night feeling like there was something I had forgotten to do, and I couldn't put my finger on what it was. I was forgetting to be in pain. That hurt stayed behind. I didn't take it with me. In the space that void consumed, the tomb of unacknowledged trauma, I needed to create something new. No longer would my existence be used for acts of war. I wanted to use myself for a form of restorative justice, and I needed to keep walking myself toward what that was going to look like.

We headed to the Jersey shore a few days later. I lounged in a chair and looked over all the skin I was used to covering up. I looked at everything and tried to be OK with all the imperfections. I took an inventory: I have a scar on my knee from falling while learning a new ice-skating skill when I was ten or so. I have a quarter-sized stamp on the back of my right calf from a friend's motorcycle muffler. I saw the freckles that were appearing everywhere, revealed by the sun. I saw the random array of multicolored bruises and the skinned shin from a failed skimboarding endeavor just that morning. I put my thumb on the tattooed birds that sit firmly atop my right thigh, the birds that can't ever leave me. I began to feel peace—real, full peace—for the first time in more than a decade. The relationship I'd had with the events in my life was beginning to change.

After a while, a new firehouse was calling my name. I felt ready to take a massive leap of faith but also stuck, sitting on the hinge of that decision. I wanted to be recovered enough to start completely over, and I also wanted to never have to speak of the pain again. I knew I could not exist within these mutually exclusive dual purposes of silence and rebellion.

But I wanted to be a living testimony, a lifelong witness to the power of resilience. I didn't know if it was possible to be someone who sometimes spoke of the pain but didn't get swept up in it again. And in order to be a living testimony, I knew I had to bear witness to my experiences. All of them.

I sat across from my good friend Carl, years of emotion heavy on my heart. I was lamenting about those conflicting feelings, talking about the worst-case scenarios if I went back to the fire service but feeling undeniably called to be there. He looked at me over his computer screen and laid it out in classic Carl fashion: "First of all, if you're going to talk about the worst-case scenario, then you also have to think about the best-case scenario. It's just as likely."

I considered this, feeling a little lighter.

"Here's the question. Do you believe you can be a firefighter again and do it as a mentally well person?"

"Yes," I said firmly.

He nodded. "So take action on that belief. Do something about it."

I felt the blossom of peaceful recognition. I was ready to act.

Carl said to me recently,

When you have experienced trauma, it's really easy to get stuck in a pattern of making decisions from a place of fear. Is that rustling in the bush actually a tiger, or is it just the memory of one? You can sit up in the trees, too scared to find out, but that is a terrible place to be. Too scared of the unknown to make a move. But when you make the move, even if it is the tiger in the bush, at least you know and can make choices. But it probably won't be. Most of the time, your head overstates the severity of the consequence. You just have to do it, find out, make choices, and then move forward. But Ali, your story is what can happen when instead of choosing fear, you chose hope.

It's so easy to believe that we are destined for the worst-case scenario, and this can become a habit. But... what if the best possible thing happens? After all, it's the stories we tell about our stories that counts. It's our interpretation of it, the meaning we make, and the choices we choose that count. Even if you've been let down time and time again, allow your relationship to your experiences to change and allow space for the belief that good things can also happen to you.

A kind voice answered the phone when I called the fire station later that day. The man on the other end was one of the chiefs at that firehouse, and after I told him a bit about myself, he invited me to come to the next weekly training. When that day came, my heart was fluttering with nervousness. The sun was beginning to set as the engine idled along the side of the station. The training scenario was to pull the hose line off the engine, haul it up the stairway, and advance it all the way to the back corner of the second floor to put out the "fire."

I volunteered to go first, wanting to get the nerves out of my system. I hoped and prayed that muscle memory would take over. I said a quick prayer and then stepped up on the diamond-plated side step of the engine. I maneuvered the "minute-man" hose load out of the hose bed, turned away from the engine with the nozzle draped down to my waist, stepped down with it on my shoulder, and began to walk toward the building. As soon as I knew I had the load balanced, I began to jog. *Drop the load, flake the hose, go on air, chalk the door, hustle up the stairs, down the hallway. Stay low, hug the wall, move with purpose.* I did it all with ease.

For the next six months, I said yes to every firefighting opportunity that came my way. I was there for every training, every workout, every week. I did that because if it was going to turn bad, if I was going to be hurt again, I wanted to know as soon as possible. It never did turn bad and never has again. Thank you, Jesus.

Every interaction was a healing, a coming home. I wanted to join an international organization called Women in Fire and needed a letter of support from my chief to do so. I was nervous to ask him, but he happily wrote one. No one there, at least not to my knowledge, cared about my gender. I was never singled out;

my boundaries were never violated. It was a firehouse unlike one I'd ever known. I felt a sense of security that had been missing for over a decade. I never stopped believing that it existed. This firehouse was the Christmas Day for one thousand Christmas Eves.

My love for firefighting had become a weight I carried always, sometimes to try to prove a point, sometimes because I didn't want to give in, sometimes because I didn't know how to let it go, but always because I deeply loved what I knew it could be. It had been so long since I carried my love for firefighting in a way that made me feel free, so long since that first cloudless October day when I put on fire gear for the first time. Even though that gear was heavy, it hadn't yet made me feel burdened. All the ways I learned to fight, all the ways I learned to blend, and all the subtle cues I'd learned to pick up on to gauge my safety just weren't needed anymore. When I dropped the weight of my love for firefighting, swam up from the bottom of my ocean, and stopped being the Sunken Girl, I'd made my peace with never stepping in a firehouse again. But here I was.

Around this time, my advocacy started to change, as my relationship with my story was changing. I'd been advocating in the standard way for a really long time, ever since *Where Hope Lives* had been published. I got onstage, and I told my story. But somewhere along the way, that just wasn't "it" anymore. I was talking about what happened to me, but that was just reacting to the broken system. I wanted to take an additional step but wasn't sure of the direction. I was speaking in every corner of the country, riding a swelling wave of interest in my story.

I was asked to keynote Women in Fire's International Conference, an organization I now sit on the board of. The large audience was almost entirely women firefighters, with a few men standing in the back. Toward the end of my talk, I looked out across the room and tried to make eye contact with as many women as I could. I told them how I had wished for them. When I felt so alone in my first firehouse, I prayed that a room full of badass women firefighters existed somewhere, that I wasn't as alone as I felt at the time. I thanked them for being my answered prayer, a realized dream. I smiled, the end.

I looked down to switch off my slide advancer, and when I looked up, every person in the room was on their feet. Their applause filled my soul with a new level of peace. I desperately needed these women to exist. I wanted to know them. I wanted them to know me. And here they were. I got to tell them everything. I told them that I was back in love with the fire service and would make sure I never fell out of love again as long as I could know them. I walked back to my seat and sat down. My dear friend and mentor jona, a fire chief in New Mexico, draped her arm across my shoulders as I leaned into her.

"We're so glad to have you back," she whispered.

Tears of relief and gratitude welled up in my eyes as I laid my head on her shoulder.

A few days later, an experience on my way to a speaking engagement caused me to post this on social media:

Yesterday I pulled into a parking space in front of a local elementary school. As I hurried up to the main entrance with my colleague, a man standing on the sidewalk called out to me. "You have a fire company license plate on your car," he stated. "Sure do," I said, still walking. "Who are you related to?" he asked, confused and slightly accusing. I knew exactly where he was going. He was asking: whose car are you driving because that license plate surely can't be for you. "I'm not related to anyone. That plate is for me." We kept walking, leaving him behind. My colleague shook her head in disbelief. "If he still thinks that a firefighter can't possibly look like you..."

It happens at the gas station when someone sees the fire gear in the back seat of my car. "Driving your dad's car?" I've been asked by a random stranger. It happened in a restaurant recently when a group of guys questioned the fire company jacket I was wearing. "Does your boyfriend know you stole his jacket?" they said jokingly.

It's happened in firehouses, big and small, metropolitan and rural, all over the country. "Whose girlfriend are you?"

I've earned every right to call myself a firefighter. I've met every standard and passed every test for more than a decade. What I look like has no effect on my ability to do that job well. When I wear my gear, I do so because it allows me to do that job and not because I fit into a fantasy that guys have of girls in firefighter Halloween costumes. I don't care that what I look like and what I do don't make sense to a lot of people. I don't do the job to prove a point or be divisive. I do it because I love it and am good at it. The End.

Instead of feeling bullied or singled out in a negative way, I was finally comfortable with the ways I stood out as a woman firefighter. I felt at home at my new firehouse, and there, my abilities and interests, like my affinity for technical rescue, were appreciated and encouraged. I invite you to find comfort in what sets you apart. This is a way we can reframe our experiences, positively changing how we view our stories even if we are in the midst of living through hard parts of them. As my entire relationship with firefighting changed, I no longer felt like I was living under this burden of struggle. I wanted to know more about how other people's relationships to their stories had changed as they found their way through their After.

A few weeks later, I met FDNY battalion chief Frank Leeb at a conference in Ohio. We were both getting sandwiches at lunch when I noticed the *FDNY* letters emblazoned on his chest. I was honored that he took a few minutes to ask about my firehouse and exchange contact information. It took me a few weeks to work up the courage to reach out and ask him to share his story with me. When he answered my FaceTime call for our scheduled talk, he was sitting in his office at his fire station. His white chief's shirt was cleanly pressed, and the gold bugle pins on his shoulders that represented his rank shone in the fluorescent lights. The heavy-accented New York City dispatcher droned in the background as they dropped tones for emergencies in other parts of the city. I asked him to tell me his story of September 11 and what his journey has been like in the many years since.

At 8:47 a.m. on September 11, 2001, the fire chief who held the position of Battalion 1 radioed to the Manhattan dispatcher that a plane had crashed into the upper floors of the World Trade Center. He asked for a fifth alarm to relocate fire companies to the area, then a few minutes later, asked for every available ambulance to be sent to what would become Ground Zero. At 8:48, the officer from Squad 18 said over the radio that it could be a "terrorist attack." How right he was. Frank wasn't working on that Tuesday but arrived in the city early that afternoon. When I asked him what the city was like that day, he thought for a few moments.

"Unified."

Just then, the dispatcher's voice boomed loudly behind him.

"Engine..."

I waited.

"Ladder..."

Frank still wasn't needed.

"Battalion!"

He hopped up from his desk, said a quick "Let me call you back," and the screen went black. I sat there for a moment, looking at my own reflection, sending him and all his firefighters thoughts of safety. The most infamous call on the most infamous day started the same way—just another problem they were tasked with fixing.

When he called me back a few minutes later, shaking his head about the fire alarm they had just gone to, Frank told me his story in detail, including the specifics of working on the pile. "The pile" refers to the 14.6-acre plot of debris on the land where the Twin Towers once stood.

"Every time we would come off the pile and go to one of the designated rest areas, I would take a few letters and read them. People sent them from all over the world, just for us. You know, the job of a firefighter changed that day. It will never be the same. I've been to firehouses all over the world, and in every single one of them, there's something about the FDNY or 9/11. It touched everybody. It changed us all."

He was golfing with his son a few days prior to our conversation when someone noticed his FDNY baseball hat and asked him if he was working on that infamous day.

"How do you feel about that?" I asked, thinking I wouldn't like a stranger asking me something so personal.

He shrugged. "At least they care to remember."

Forrest and I went to the 9/11 Memorial & Museum that Christmas. We descended underground and walked the massive footprints of the towers, standing on the mass grave. We looked at the enormous pieces of twisted steel that had split, melted, and curled away from the airplane-shaped bombs. We looked up at the pictures—the sea of thousands of faces whose lives ended on the same day. I stood for a long time staring at the crushed remains of FDNY's Ladder 3 and thought of the eleven firefighters who rode that piece of apparatus into Ground Zero, almost twice the usual amount due to it being shift change and everyone piling on when the call came in. Not one of those firefighters survived.

On that day, when war came to Lower Manhattan, in the midst of the initial panic, before the "why" of it all was known, the emergency service workers did not hesitate. They just did what they'd been doing for decades and tried to bring order to that unimaginable chaos. But in just a few moments, however long it took for the towers to come down, they were gone. Dust. Three hundred and forty-three firefighters. Centuries of combined experience. Decades of an institutional love. They were giants. Living legends. If I'm ever feeling defeated because I love a job that has not wanted me and I'm looking for a reason to believe in the goodness of firefighters, I don't have to look any further than that day in September.

As each year passes, those who witnessed the tragedy of September 11 gain more time away from that experience. But due to all those who continue to die from 9/11-related illnesses, the trauma is still being perpetuated decades later, and emotional distance isn't easily found. How do you begin to change your relationship to your story when you still have to show up for funerals? It's still possible, but the work must be that much more intentional.

That spring, I was listening to the *My Favorite Murder* podcast when I heard the hosts retell a survival story that had happened a few days earlier. Through social media, I sought out the brand-new survivor, and I've been so privileged in the time since to become her friend.

On March 5, 2017, in Seattle, Washington, around one in the afternoon, Kelly Herron was four miles into her thirteen-mile run. It was her tenth week of training for a marathon, and everything was going perfectly. She had not missed a single day, she was stretching enough, her feet didn't hurt. All was as it should be.

As she approached the Golden Gardens Park, she stopped to snap a few pictures, as she often did when she ran. A woman with her small dog and a few teenagers were skipping rocks across the sandy beach. The bathroom was an unassuming brown building set back on the shore. As she jogged up to it, she was looking forward to a reprieve from the thirty-eight-degree weather and freezing rain and wind. A year ago, she had stopped to use this same bathroom and had paused her GPS, which caused it to incorrectly record her run in two sections. This time, she consciously kept it recording as she walked in. Kelly described that bathroom as "something you'd find in a prison. Three stalls, no mirrors, a dirty concrete floor."

After using the bathroom, she took an extra second to warm her hands under the hand dryer, allowing her fingers to thaw. Suddenly, Kelly felt that something was wrong.

I first talked with Kelly through FaceTime on a hot night in late July, coming up on five months since the day of her attack. She told me her story in great detail, often incredulously retelling what happened to her.

During our first conversation, Kelly's ever-present laugh was a genuine reflection of that intact spirit. She told me that three weeks before the attack, she'd taken a self-defense class that her work offered.

"I'd been putting it off for weeks and then at the last second, I went."

During the class, she'd asked extra questions about what to do in certain situations, thinking of all the times she spent running alone in isolated areas.

"After what happened, people said that I was lucky." She shook her head adamantly against that assumption, her ponytail swinging. "I was not lucky. I was prepared."

Turning around to leave the bathroom, she was startled by the presence of a man standing directly behind her, ominously silent. She apologized immediately, thinking she was incorrectly in the men's room. The next second, he lunged at her, arms outstretched.

She told me, "I wasn't even scared initially. I was really sure that I was going to get away from him and run out of there. It didn't register."

Unable to escape his grasp, he pulled her back into the stall he had been hiding in. He later confessed to police that he'd be waiting for someone to use the hand dryer so he "could rape them." Instantly on her stomach with him on top of her, she started throwing her elbows back. Her assailant—already classified as a level-three sex offender who had attacked another woman just weeks before—was wearing an oversized sweatshirt, so her punches failed to connect with anything but the fabric that was hanging off his 5'11" frame. She joked that the expensive Lululemon running pants she had on coupled with the rainy weather made her like a wet seal.

"He could not get a grasp on my pants to pull them off," she explained. Kelly and her attacker continued to wrestle and wound up laying side-by-side on the grimy, cold, sand-covered floor. A primal defiance rose up inside of her.

"I have never been so angry in my entire life," she told me, drawing out the words for emphasis.

She paused in reflection. "Another thing about me: I am two years sober."

I smiled, humbled by another detail of her story.

"I have fought so hard for my life. So hard. Everything was going so well, and here this asshole was about to ruin it."

Seething with anger, furious and fuming, Kelly bellowed into his face, "Not today, motherfucker!"

I smiled at the battle cry that had gone viral.

"It seemed to catch him off guard," she mused with a grin.

The ear warmers Kelly had on to protect against the frigid rain caused all of this to sound muted, until her scream echoed in her head.

"Did he say anything to you? Did he say anything at all?" I asked.

She shook her head.

"It was the weirdest thing. He didn't make so much as a grunt the whole time. Not even when I scratched his face and made him bleed."

As he tried to pin her to the ground, she started striking him in the head with the side of her arm, as she learned to do in her self-defense class. She wiggled away and got into the next stall over. The self-defense instructor said that whatever you think you should do in the moment like that, just do it. Don't question your instinct, just do it. Trust yourself.

Lying on her back, she glanced up at the closed but unlocked stall door. She thought that if she could lock that door and put a barrier in between them, it could buy her a little time to escape. Following her gut, she shot her foot up and it connected solidly with the lock. The adrenaline coursing through her body caused her to kick the lock with such force that it jammed the door into the side of the stall, unable to be moved. Undeterred, her attacker slid under the side of the stall and got on top of her. He started punching her in the face repeatedly.

Fighting to stay conscious, Kelly reached her arms up and pulled herself around the front of the stall, slicing her head open at her eyebrow, cutting it on the bottom of the closed door. Seconds away from losing consciousness from the blows to her head, feeling completely and utterly exhausted, Kelly stood up on shaky legs, feeling like she did not have any more fight left in her.

"I knew that if I passed out, I was going to get raped. He was going to rape me in that disgusting bathroom, on that sandy floor, while I had dirt in my mouth."

With the door—freedom—in her periphery, Kelly heard a voice in her head say, *Kelly, hang in there. You are almost out of this.* She lunged for the door and burst forth into the fresh air.

"I came flying out of the bathroom, bleeding and sweating, and there were three people standing there looking at me ... doing ... nothing."

My mouth dropped open for the first time.

"It really pisses me off that all the news articles said people came running to my aid. That's a complete lie. I yelled at these people, 'Couldn't you fucking hear me?!'"

The lady with the dog just stared at her. "Well, I didn't have a phone," she countered.

"You could at least have opened the door!" Kelly screamed.

Someone called 9-1-1 for her and Kelly talked to the dispatcher. She was proud of herself for being able to describe her attacker correctly, except for thinking he was a huge man.

"It certainly felt that way," she reasoned.

Knowing he was still in the bathroom, Kelly searched for a way to lock him in there until the police arrived. A passerby gave her a carabiner, which she used to secure the outside door.

"He was still in the stall with the jammed door when the police got there. He didn't even try to escape. The police had to break down the stall door to get him out."

When they did, he told them to just "kill him."

It was only then that she thought to turn off her GPS watch. It had recorded her fight in that building, the jagged red line becoming another part of her viral fame.

Kelly and I have become fast friends in the years since we first spoke. In the time since, she's endured flashbacks, testified against her attacker, and seen him put in jail. Her relationship with running evolved. She moved across the county and got married. I interviewed her again recently and asked for her thoughts on her journey, now a few years after her attack.

"At first, my recovery was like a boomerang. I would feel OK, like I was over it and good, and then I would have to grieve again." She looked at me through FaceTime as she sat in her car, a pandemic-mandatory bandana hanging around her neck.

"In that first year, I set deadlines. I ran a race four months after the attack and had my mind made up that as soon as I crossed the finish line, I would leave the trauma behind. That, of course, did not happen. A few months later, I ran the full marathon that I'd been training for, and crossing that finish line still did not heal me. There was a huge sense of relief in doing it, but I wasn't all better."

Kelly endured a terrible flashback while running that race. She was startled by a male runner, and she saw his face transform into her attacker's.

The court case took an entire year, and I vividly remember her agonizing over it all. When Kelly testified against her attacker in court and read her victim impact statement, she said to the judge, "When I left him in that bathroom, I left him in a room that had nothing but a sink and a toilet. I'm asking you to do the same."

The judge sentenced the offender to the maximum sentence that being found guilty of felony assault with sexual motivation carries: an insulting three years. The judge then asked Kelly if she'd ever run the marathon she'd been training for, and Kelly replied, "Yes I did, Your Honor!"

Kelly reflected on this to me: "When I said that, I was overcome with the strongest emotion that I honestly couldn't name right away. It was joy. I hadn't felt it since the attack. I didn't even recognize it. That was the proudest day of my life. I finally felt like the badass girl from the bathroom."

Kelly ran the same race again the year her attacker was sentenced, and this time, she felt a transformative peace come over her. When she finished that Saturday, she told her mom that she felt like she had finally left her attacker behind. That Monday, Kelly was told that her attacker had died in jail the previous Friday, the day before she'd run her race.

"It's strange to be happy that someone is dead, but I truly believe he was always going to be a danger to women. He was already a repeat offender. I knew I was going to have to go before the prison board and essentially retestify every time his sentence was up to ensure that he was never released."

Kelly remembers feeling like that kept her in her own type of jail.

"I don't know how he died, and I don't really care. He's gone. It's done."

Like so many who become famous for their survival, Kelly became a very public face immediately. She became a sponsored runner, which then obligated her to tell her story constantly in interviews. As her relationship with running and what it now means for her has evolved, Kelly has arrived at a conclusion that I've watched her walk toward for the past few years.

"I don't want to tell my story anymore. At least not right now. And if I do, I want it to be on my terms in ways that feel organic."

Kelly had been offered book deals to write her story but turned them down. More and more lately, she'd been turning down interviews too. I'd been watching her bravely set boundaries around her experience, reform her identity, change her relationship to her story, and assert control over her life.

"I am forward-facing now," she told me. "I am ready to get married to the love of my life, who I met as a direct result of sharing my story. I want to run because I really like it, not because I have to. And I'm always going to be an advocate for women and runners' safety, but I'm just done talking about that day, at least for now. Thank you for writing my story so I don't have to."

That is the beautifully transformative nature of remembering our ability to choose and allowing how we feel about our stories to change. As survivors, we so often forget that we have that ability. When someone else's will is forced upon us, when the basic human ability to *choose* is overridden, we often forget that we can have choices ever again. Trauma separates by design. It separates us away from so many things, including our ability to decide, but Kelly made the most empowering decision available to her. She decided that her story was hers to tell, on her terms, and for an unforeseen period of time, she doesn't want to tell it anymore. I'm so proud of you, Kelly, and I am truly honored to share your story here.

You don't owe anyone else any part of your story unless you want to freely give it. Let me say that again: *You don't owe anyone else any part of your story unless you want to freely give it.* You get to choose how you define your experiences, and that is allowed to change as you grow away from them. Take it from Kelly—she found power as a brand-new survivor in standing in her story and owning it. Testifying before the judge made her feel empowered and joyous. Then slowly, she decided that she didn't want to be the "girl from the bathroom" anymore. She just wanted to be Kelly. She redefined and restoried. She remembered her ability to choose.

Or take it from me. I fell in love with the fire service at sixteen and thought it was going to be a home for me forever. I was right, but it just ended up looking different than I thought it would as I paved my own path and created my own space in this world. My overcoming would have been no less real if I never went back to the fire service after my PTSD diagnosis. My overcoming would have been no less valid if I never told the full story to anyone other than Jill or anyone other than myself.

As you grow away from trauma, it's natural to feel sad over the things you missed out on while you were busy surviving. Some of those experiences can't ever be had again. I used to spend energy mourning what I didn't get to do during high school and college because I was so busy surviving and was barely noticing the pieces of me that were fracturing away. It's important to let ourselves grieve what we missed out on. It doesn't mean we regret where we are; it just means that part of allowing our relationship to our stories to change includes allowing ourselves to feel all the feelings that come with our experiences. Can we look back at our younger selves and see where we could have made different choices? Sure. But don't judge the choices you made to survive.

The words I've used to tell my story have changed over time as I found more meaning and grew in my overcoming. Your relationship with your story is allowed to change as you do. I no longer see myself as a victim, and I don't tell my story from that perspective anymore. But I still tell it. I redefined and restoried. Take it from either Kelly or me—or do something else entirely. That's up to you.

REFLECTION AND ACTION

Truth #6 for Overcoming:
Your Relationship to Your
Story Will Change over Time

As we grow, we can feel restrained by the identity we first created to cope with our experiences. Release yourself from that limitation. How can you redefine and restory? What moments would you like to grieve? How has your relationship with your story changed over time?

7

DON'T PLAY THE TRAUMA OLYMPICS

It is not a question of if you will survive this, but what beautiful things await you when you do. . . . Good and bad things come from the universe holding hands. Wait for the good to come.

—Chanel Miller

I was asked to speak to inmates at a maximum-security prison near my hometown. These men were in jail for life for committing violent crimes against women. As I was led through multiple sets of locked doors, the body alarm I'd been given felt heavy in my back pocket. Flanked by two guards, I walked along a path into the chapel.

Once inside, I was directed to stand up front behind a wooden podium. I was instructed to, under no circumstances, answer any questions asked. I looked at the staff who had taken their seats in the back of the chapel as the incarcerated men filed in. I didn't know if I'd be able to look them in the eye. I don't like standing up front, alone, while audience members file in, so I sat down in the front pew. I heard them shuffle in and take their seats. When it got quiet, I glanced back at a guard, who nodded.

I stood up and gripped the small podium in front of me. Then, worried they could sense that tension, I laid my hands flat on its wooden surface. I was introduced as a crime victim, as a survivor who was going to tell her story about overcoming trauma. As I opened my mouth to say hi, I first looked at the doors at the back of the chapel, but then found my nerve and looked into the eyes of a man sitting in the front row. His orange jumpsuit cast a pallor on his face. He had long hair, dark eyes, and a well-trimmed beard. His face was kind but closed off, quiet. He was listening. I spoke for about an hour and began my closing thoughts.

"I think that's why telling my story matters. My abuse wasn't from a romantic partner, a random stranger, or a family member. It also wasn't a onetime event. It was years and years of experiences, and from an entire organization, an entire belief system. It was systemic sexism and purposeful abuse."

I paused, feeling strong and no longer intimidated by their gazes.

"It took me years to find the words to tell my story. I'm still finding them. I'm learning how to not compare my experiences to other people's either. I really appreciate you listening to me today."

There was respectful applause. Then one of the men raised his hand. I expected one of the guards to come up and dismiss them, but no one moved. I looked to the guard who told me not to answer any questions, and he shrugged, which I took as "go for it."

I nodded, and the young man with his hand raised asked a thoughtful question: "In your experience working with those who have been abused and knowing about those who hurt them, what is the one quality you know of in abusers that means they have the ability to change?"

I wondered who he had hurt and if he'd gone as far as taking someone's life.

I told him, "The only quality that will lead anyone to make change is whether or not they are willing to take responsibility for their actions. Owning what they've done; not passing the blame to anything or anyone else. If you've done something that you now regret, you did it because you chose to. Not for any other reason. Making change means making different choices altogether."

After visiting the prison, I found myself discounting my experiences because, as I thought about those who were victims of these men's crimes, my story was so "mild" comparatively. But that doesn't mean that what happened to me was insignificant. We always have the right to be impacted by events and share our stories independent of what's happened to other people.

One day, a calm, low voice played in my voice mail box.

"Hi, Ali, my name is Jim, and I am a survivor of the January 8, 2011, shooting in Tucson, Arizona, that injured Gabrielle Giffords."

He and I spoke late on a Friday night, due to the time difference between Philadelphia and Arizona. He told me his story with humility and appreciation for both his health and the health of his wife. As a fire prevention specialist with a long history of firefighters in his family, we got to know each other through talking about the job we had both found our way in. Jim told me that the shooting was the third event in a trifecta of traumas that had happened in the years leading up to that day. His cancer diagnosis in 2009 brought a medical crisis to his family, then one year later, their house was robbed while he and his wife were in bed asleep. The shooting happened on an ordinary Saturday, but it became an event that the people of Tucson would carry forever, the tragedy of it settling into the soil of the landscape.

"I did not see the shooter," Jim told me. "I had my head slightly down, eyes closed as I was preparing what I wanted to say to the congresswoman."

As an instructor at the National Fire Academy, he wanted to encourage her to support the organization through upcoming budgets and legislation. But he never got a single word out.

"I didn't see him coming. He walked in front of me, pulled a Glock out from under his hoodie, and just shot her. There was no time to do anything at all."

Around 10:10 a.m., just after shooting the congresswoman, the shooter turned his gun on Jim. Standing just three feet away, Jim took a shot to the right side of his upper chest, which knocked him backward. It blew a two-inch hole in his right clavicle, severing nerves to his shoulder, arm, and hand. As the bullet ricocheted through his body, it splintered apart, breaking into three pieces that all came to rest in various places around his spine, including one that knocked into his right vocal cord. As he fell backward, he was hit with another bullet that entered and exited his lower right leg. Jim hit the concrete hard as blood began to pour from his six-foot-two, three-hundred-pound body.

"It was an utterly helpless feeling," he told me. "I was hearing people get shot around me, and I was unable to do anything about it."

Seventeen seconds later, the extended clip of the gun was empty of its bullets. As the shooter attempted to reload, bystanders wrestled the magazine and then the gun away from him. One bystander threw a chair at the shooter and punched him in the face, which is why he has a black eye in his mugshot. They had him subdued as 9-1-1 calls began to flood into the dispatch center.

Jim lay flat on his back, looking up at the roof overhang in front of the grocery store, unable to move. Trying to stay conscious and breathing, his eyes focused on the sprinkler heads that hung down out of the ceiling, a fixture his profession made him very familiar with. This recognizable and comforting site brought him back to reality. His wife was crouched eight feet away, miraculously uninjured.

The cashier, who had sold the shooter a bottle of water just a few minutes earlier, came rushing out of the Safeway with some butcher's whites from the deli to staunch people's bleeding. As Jim's wife and two other women knelt by his side, taking off his belt to use as a tourniquet around his leg, he could feel someone unknowingly kneel on his fingers. Doris crouched down and held her ear to his lips, noticing that he was trying to speak.

"Can you please . . . ask the kind lady to get off my fingers?" He chuckled as he told me this part, reminiscing. "The fact that I could feel anything at all seemed like a really good sign."

Five minutes after the last shot was fired, police officers arrived on the scene, arrested the shooter, and took control. Paramedics arrived one minute later. Jim tried to stay awake as an ambulance rushed him to the closest hospital. Finally, in the emergency department at the University of Arizona's Medical Center, Jim let himself fade into unconsciousness, telling himself that he and his wife were finally safe.

Three days after the shooting, Doris briefly left Jim's side to go home and change purses. Reaching into the outer pocket of the blue purse she'd been holding since Saturday, she pulled out a bullet casing. The next day, she handed it to the FBI agent and deputy sheriff at the hospital, who exclaimed in disbelief.

"The thirty-third bullet!"

They had combed the scene for evidence and found thirty-two bullet casings from the extended clip but knew there had been an additional bullet in the chamber. The missing casing exited the gun and landed in the outer pocket of Doris's purse. That's how close she was to the shooter. She'd been carrying the casing around with her for three days.

I asked Jim if he has found closure in the years since the shooting. He disagreed with the word *closure*, saying that January 8, 2011, is a day that will be with him forever:

> I do not have full use of my right arm; I have chronic pain; my vocal cord is permanently damaged and caused me to resign my contract instructor position at the National Fire Academy. So I do not have closure, as this event

will never leave me. But I do have resolution. I remember lying in that hospital bed. The doctors had cut two large incisions around the wound in my leg so I didn't get compartment syndrome; my body ached; I was in an incredible amount of pain. I realized in that moment that I had a choice to make. A quote from the longtime head basketball coach of UCLA, the late John Wooden, came to me: "There is a choice you have to make in everything you do. So keep in mind that in the end, the choice you make makes you." This quote really stuck with me. My faith, my sense of humor, and my existing coping skills all contributed to my recovery.

Anyone in any sort of proximity to this incident might have felt some impact from this trauma, ranging from symptoms that lasted for a couple of days to those that stuck around and could result in a PTSD diagnosis. But those who had a loved one in the area might also experience trauma from the incident—even those who shop at the same chain of grocery stores might have found themselves feeling traumatized from what happened. The details of the trauma don't change, but the way each person perceives it through their paradigm and makes meaning of it is as unique as we are.

In *The 7 Habits of Highly Effective People*, Stephen Covey tells us that "paradigms are powerful because they create the lens through which we see the world." Each person's perspective is as real to them as yours is to you. The meaning that we make out of any sort of event is valid based on our individual life experiences up to and including the moment of trauma. Paradigms often change after a traumatic experience, as our understanding of what can happen to us expands our worldview.

In my work with 9-1-1 dispatchers, I've found that some think that because they are not physically on the scene, they have "no right" to feel any post-traumatic stress. When I teach clinicians about the culture of the emergency services, we listen to many different 9-1-1 calls, including those from the Columbine and Sandy Hook shootings, those who were on the phone with 9/11 victims as they perished in the World Trade Center attack, and calls involving domestic violence, lost children, drownings, and mass casualty incidents. I don't know what counts as exposure to trauma if not that. Trauma can come from your emotional proximity to something, not necessarily your physical proximity to it. But so often, first responders, trauma survivors, and others dismiss their experience by ranking it against those who were closest to death, as if that's the only thing that counts.

After speaking at a university one evening, a college student was waiting for me as I gathered my things to leave the auditorium. Speaking as if she couldn't believe she was saying the words out loud, she told me that she'd been sexually assaulted as a child. She said the experience was "eating her alive," and she had never told another person until me. She was understandably still very affected by the incident for many reasons, but even more so by the burden of keeping the secret, of feeling like she would be thought of as broken, dirty, or at fault somehow. She didn't think that what happened to her was "bad enough" to warrant help.

We talked about what resources were available for her on campus, and I sent her out of the auditorium prepared to use one of them. She was finally ready to release herself from the burden of bearing the secret of something that never should have happened to her in the first place.

At a conference in Pennsylvania about trauma and the resources in the state, I heard an unbelievable story of loss that could have been irrevocably crippling and permanently consuming. But there she was, the holder of an impossible loss, standing strong in front of us that morning at the conference center.

Lynn told us about her ten-year-old daughter and her eight-year-old son, the ages they will be forever. Jennifer and David were murdered by their father, Lynn's ex-husband, on Christmas Day in 1994. I then heard her friend, grief counselor Lisa, speak about grief in a way I'd never heard before. Lynn and Lisa have coauthored an impactful self-help book called *Grief: The Event, the Work, the Forever.*

After hearing her story, I knew I wanted to talk with her more about the journey she'd been on since Christmas Day 1994. Lynn spoke to me twenty-five years after her children were murdered, shortly after their birthday weeks. Jennifer would have been thirty-five and David would have been thirty-four.

While we spoke, Lynn's soft but strong voice conveyed profound truths about domestic violence, crime, and trauma. I've compiled her words from her TED Talk presentation, book, and what she shared with me to tell you some of her story here. I am honored to play a small part in keeping the memory of her children alive. She looked at me through FaceTime as her new kitten tiptoed playfully across her desk.

"Domestic violence honors no sanctuary. It does not discriminate."

Lynn had been married to a man who'd started abusing her almost immediately. He called her fat and ugly and told her that no one else would ever love her. He repeatedly raped her. He made her sleep under the watchful eye of a security camera that was always trained on her. He put a bar across her steering wheel so she couldn't drive when he didn't give her permission to and made her strip down upon entering their house so he could do a full-body inspection.

"He had me completely isolated. I was too humiliated about it all to tell my family."

Lynn knew that she couldn't take the treatment forever but was so sure that she could not support herself and the children on her $20,000 annual salary. She tried to hang on until they were older. But in their ninth year of marriage, Lynn's husband tried to strangle her to death, and she knew that this had to be enough. Through their divorce proceedings, she requested supervised visitation for the kid's father, but the judge refused.

"I'll never forget the judge's words. He said, 'Mother, just because he hurt you doesn't mean he'll hurt the children.'"

Eighteen months later was Christmas Eve 1994. Lynn dropped Jennifer and David off to spend the night with their father and his family. Lynn and her then boyfriend, now husband, Paul, were to pick them up the next morning. On Christmas Day, having no luck contacting her ex-husband, Lynn and Paul arrived at the house. Looking in the front window, they saw blood on the floor in the living room. Paul sat Lynn on the front curb facing away from the house and went next door to ask the neighbor to go in with him to look for the children. Paul first came upon their father dead on the couch, then found David and Jennifer in their beds upstairs, covered in blood, having been fatally stabbed. Their father had written a checklist summing up the plan he'd been forming for more than a year as his grasp on reality loosened. "Kill Jennifer and David" was the last item on the to-do list. After killing his children, their father then killed himself.

I was completely taken with Lynn's ability to move through her grief and make meaning out of it. Lynn eventually worked with the Pennsylvania Office of Victim Services before retiring from that job after twenty years. Lynn spoke to me of the fear that initially gripped her for years, of the feeling of being desperately suicidal that she could not shake.

"At the time of their murder, I was collapsed with grief. Suicidal. I simply did not think I could go on," Lynn said.

Lynn told me about her turning point. Ten or so years after her children were murdered, she had spoken at an event and, as usual, some people came up to her afterward to share their stories.

"A woman said that she had something in common with me. She was sobbing, completely beside herself. She told me that her child had also been murdered. I remember looking at her and thinking that it was way too soon for her to be at a conference like this. Her emotions were so raw, I assumed that the murder must have been recent."

Lynn shook her head as she walked me through her realization.

"It turned out that her child had been murdered the year Jennifer was born, 1984. I looked at her and thought, *This can't be me in another ten or twenty years. I have to find my way through this. I can't let him take more of my life.* There is no such thing as closure. Time doesn't heal, but it helps you figure out how to weave the event into your life. We have to get more comfortable talking about death, especially the tragic ones."

"Over time, I have found a new identity and purpose. The murder of Jen and Dave doesn't define me," she said. "And I've lost lots of friends because of that. I have to remind others that I am other things now. Crime and trauma [do] not consume or control my life anymore, but sometimes people still see me as that person in grief."

We talked about how the words we find to share our stories change and evolve over time. "Some people don't even catch that I was sexually assaulted until they hear me speak because it's not specifically said in *Where Hope Lives*," I told her.

"I didn't know until I heard your TED Talk," Lynn agreed.

I shrugged. "I used the words I had at the time." Lynn nodded in understanding. I smiled. "I have a lot more words now."

On the same day that I met Lynn, I met Frank DeAngelis, who was the principal at Columbine High School during the April 1999 shooting. As he took his place at the front of the conference room to speak to us, he began by reciting the names of the dead—his voice strong, grieving, and defiant all at once.

A Columbine is actually the Colorado state flower, but in the twenty-plus years since the shooting there, that word has become synonymous with violence. The Columbine High School shooting was a mostly failed bombing, but inside of just one hour, twelve students and one teacher were killed or fatally wounded and twenty-six others were injured. It was the first time that a tragedy like this had been so witnessed. The Columbine shooting was before smartphones and social media, but the two bodies lying outside, the rescue of survivors, and the lengthy process of securing the school were all livestreamed on national television. It was the first time America watched students run from their school with their hands over their heads. Eventually, the news cycle continued on as it does, and the media left Littleton, Colorado, spreading many myths about this incident, many of which continue on to this day.

But the Columbine story did not begin or end on April 20, 1999, nor is its stamp on history entirely one of tragedy. The Columbine community's legacy of perseverance, resilience, and leadership in action was already set in motion due to many factors but particularly due to one man: Columbine High School's beloved principal Frank DeAngelis.

On April 20, 1999, at 11:19 in the morning, Frank was alerted by his assistant to the report of gunfire in their school. The fire alarm was sounding and the strobe lights were flashing. The school was descending into panic with different groups being aware of the danger to varying degrees. Frank ran out of his office, unsure of what was going on, hoping that this was a senior prank. Hearing a commotion down the hall, Frank turned to see one of his students walking toward him. This student had a rifle in his hands. The gunman fired at Frank but missed, shattering the glass doors in the entryway directly behind him. Just then, a group of about twenty-five girls entered that hallway, unaware that they were between Frank and a student with a gun. Frank rushed them into a side hallway and to a door, but due to the school being in the preliminary stages of lockdown, that door was locked.

On the other side of it was help: a Jefferson County sheriff. Frank knew that the gunmen were behind them, right around the corner. He reached into his pocket for the massive ring of about thirty-five unmarked, similar keys that could open most doors in the school. And in that moment, something happened that hadn't happened before or since. Frank reached for the correct key on the first try and led those girls to safety. It later came to light that Frank's good friend and teacher Dave Sanders came into the hallway at that moment and distracted the gunmen so Frank could get himself and the girls out. Dave died in the school several hours later due to blood loss from his gunshot wounds, despite the efforts of many students to save his life.

The work of trauma recovery happens outside of the moment, in the After. Survivorship begins immediately. In these moments, we have opportunities to choose—to choose our response, to choose who we are going to be. Frank made a choice to show up and lead his community despite being incredibly traumatized and unsure of how to continue on in his grief. Frank continued to show up to work for fourteen years after the shooting to show students, parents, and staff that they didn't need to be afraid to come to school, that they could reclaim that place as theirs. He remained as principal until every single student who was in his school district at the time of the shooting, even those who were in preschool, graduated from high school. Now retired, Frank is a resource for educators, first responders, and safety officials before and after they experience a shooting, and he travels internationally to tell Columbine's story.

When I met Frank, I was captivated by his honesty, his determination to not forget the "Beloved Thirteen," and his resolve to do what he can to prevent other communities from experiencing a similar tragedy. What we can all learn from Frank is not just what he did on the day of the shooting or even in the immediate aftermath but what he has done every day since.

In addition to Frank, I met Heather, a student at Columbine who had hidden in a closet for hours during the shooting. Heather heard gunshots as Frank was rushing outside. Each person's experience on that day was wholly separate yet intertwined. If you wanted to rank their trauma, you might do so based on their proximity to the flying bullets, to the gunmen, to death. But what about those who hid for hours and never saw a gun? Those who stayed home from school sick that day as their classmates were murdered? Is their trauma less valid? It should never be a competition of who suffered more: trauma is trauma. What about the parents who had to sit in limbo for hours as they waited for news on their child? What about those who lost friends versus those who didn't? Every single person experienced the day differently but is no less valid in the trauma they experienced.

With my mind always on the emergency services, I thought about those who responded to incidents of mass violence. I thought of those who responded to the murder of Lynn's children, who carefully removed their little bodies from their beds, performed their autopsies, buried them. Who helped them process that event?

I knew there were teams that provide crisis counseling to first responders following a critical incident. I found the local critical incident stress management group online and signed up for the training, sure this was a new path I was meant to be on.

I trained in individual and group counseling through the International Critical Incident Stress Foundation. I trained with firefighters, medics, police officers, and dispatchers. We learned about critical incident stress management and how exactly to help first responders after a traumatic incident. It made me think of my very first fire call and the lack of care and resources that were available for us. I waited for an opportunity to use my training.

That moment came when my phone rang early in the morning a few weeks before Christmas. On the other end was the coordinator of the CISM team. She spoke in stressed fragments.

"House fire, two kids dead, they're still in the house, lots of first responders still there, can you get to the scene? Now?"

Forrest helped me get ready, but I hurried out the door without thinking of much else. I arrived on the scene not sure what to expect. Both parents and the daughter escaped; the dad was badly burned from trying to rescue his sons.

When I arrived, I hung back and looked at every emergency worker's face, trying to name the feelings I saw on each, to make sure I was a face of calm. I looked up at the bedroom window of the house, picturing the little boys whose bodies were still in there and the Christmas presents that had been tucked under the tree for them. I shuttled coffee back and forth from the warming tent, knowing there were no words that I could say but taking the opportunity to connect when I delivered it. I remembered what I had learned about the "gift of presence" from my friend James and a firefighter/ chaplain friend Jeremy. Standing there with these first responders, experiencing a bit of the trauma with them, being willing to not look away from the body bags, and just being there was what was needed. The time for words would come later.

Firefighters stood in a line, holding up tarps so the boys in their body bags would be shielded from the news cameras. A drone flew overhead, giving the detectives and medical examiner's office a bird's-eye view of the burned-out house, since, due to the deaths, it was a crime scene. Six hours later, I left, cold to the bone, exhausted but so incredibly grateful that I could be there to help.

Those who had attempted to rescue the boys—despite the flames that had already consumed that part of the house—experienced the event in one way; those who had arrived on the scene afterward had felt a different type of dread; those who responded later and simply stood by as the medical examiners worked had yet a different experience. They all experienced the trauma, but in different ways. Each experience mattered, and each experience deserved to be felt and processed.

That incident gave me the opportunity to truly cut my teeth in critical incident stress management, to witness grief in its many stages, and to be a part of normalizing those reactions. More than anything I said or did as a part of those conversations, I will always remember the extraordinary sense of gratitude I felt to be able to sit in sadness with others, to simply to keep them company there, without trying to change anything that they were feeling or rush their process.

Toxic positivity has no place in trauma recovery. "Toxic positivity is the assumption, either by one's self or others, that despite a person's emotional pain or difficult situation, they should only have a positive mindset," explains Dr. Jaime Zuckerman. No "good vibes only." No "but it happened for a reason," and absolutely no "other people have it worse; you're so lucky." When I spoke with Jill recently, she noted that I was very much in that toxically positive space when we first started our work together. She said that I had the instinct to want to skip the severity and significance of my experiences and go right to the overcoming. We might think, *What's wrong with being positive?* In this context, forced positivity is an act of dismissing the pain that is demanding to be felt and bypassing the work that must be done to genuinely arrive at a place where we can reflect back from a more positive place.

Much of the work surrounding trauma recovery has to do with making meaning out of what has happened to us. The meaning we make directly relates to the validity we give to our reaction to the trauma or the way we've framed it in our minds. Do we see ourselves as a victim that only bad things happen to? Do we judge ourselves for being impacted in the way that we have? Are we constantly ranking our reaction against other peoples'? Playing these Trauma Olympics prevents us from making that meaning and finding our resilience. In her article "How Resilience Works," Diane Coutu tells us that "this dynamic of meaning making is, most researchers agree, the way resilient people build bridges from present-day hardships to a fuller, better constructed future. Those bridges make the present manageable, for lack of a better word, removing the sense that the present is overwhelming."

As the reality of the situation in my first firehouse became clear, I had an experience that bolstered my ability to build that bridge. It was the middle of the night, and I'd been asleep for hours. In an instant, I awoke and sat straight up in bed. I must have been dreaming, but I felt fully awake, looking out into the darkness of my bedroom. In front of me, I saw an audience sitting at conference tables, listening. I looked down and saw myself standing at a podium. I sensed that I'd been sharing the lessons I'd learned from the adversity I was living through. It felt like I was staring into my future. I never forgot that experience because it allowed the present to become a bit more manageable.

Your story matters. The End. Period. Forever. Someone else will always have more burden to bear, but that doesn't mean that your burden isn't heavy. I used to think that my experience with sexual assault didn't count because I wasn't raped; I've even had extended family members say this to me. If you've had lots of practice dismissing your story, and if you've always been invalidated in the significance of it, this is going to seem like a big leap. But here's the plain truth: If something has impacted you, it counts as something that was impactful. If you were hurt, it counts. If you've never told anyone else what happened to you, it still matters.

REFLECTION AND ACTION

**Truth #7 for Overcoming:
Don't Play the Trauma Olympics**

Take five minutes today—perhaps first thing in the morning or before you fall asleep—to think, journal, or meditate on the following phrase: *I affirm that my experiences matter, despite how they compare with others. I am able to choose my future and am capable of taking the steps to get there.*

8

FORGIVING DOESN'T MEAN FORGETTING

Eventually you have to stop just pulling people out of the water. You have to go upstream to figure out why they are falling in in the first place.

—*Desmond Tutu*

In early 2018, I stood up in front of an audience of firefighters in a North Carolina conference room and decided that this would be the last time I told my story. I'd been telling my story publicly for eight years and felt like I wanted to advocate for change in some other way but wasn't sure how. Without a clear way forward, I thought I should take some time off to figure out what I wanted to do next.

I said everything I ever wanted to say about my story during that presentation. I held nothing back, which is how I speak still to this day. I was sure that at some point, I was going to say something that was too much or something that would make the fire service turn on me again, and so to protect myself, I didn't get really invested in myself as a speaker. I took every talk very seriously and gave 100 percent but just didn't expect for that to have a role in my life forever. It seemed too perfect, too much of a happy ending. In North Carolina on that day, I spoke for over an hour, and as my allotted time started to run out, I paused. What came out of my mouth next felt important, but at the time, I had no idea just how important. It's what I had been walking toward since my very first fire call, the little girl with the butterfly clips on the ends of her braids:

> What if instead of just reacting to firefighter suicides and assaults in firehouses . . . what if we actually went back and talked about why those things happen in the first place? What if we don't just talk about mental health when we lose someone or during mental health awareness month, but all year long? What if we can actually work toward a fire service that has space for and values everyone? What if in the shock of a line of duty death is not the first time you learned about grief? What if after holding a dead child is not the first time you learn about trauma?

After I stepped off stage, my brain kept going. What if I could make my training easily accessible not just to the chiefs and officers that sit in front of me at conferences but to a firefighter at three o'clock in the morning who just got back from a bad call? A firefighter who was struggling with the environment at their station? What if? *What if?*

In that exact moment, I realized that this was the point of everything I'd been doing since writing *Where Hope Lives.* That was where my advocacy wanted to go. I wanted to stop reacting to bad things happening; I wanted to go figure out why they happen in the first place and, even more so, give people the tools to prevent them from happening.

I figured that this would be met with a flat-out no. Our society often holds this kind of space for survivors, and I expected to be met with the following stipulations:

You can tell your story, but don't make people uncomfortable.

You can tell your story, but don't take up too much space.

You can tell your story passionately but not angrily.

You can tell your story, but don't ask for too much.

Instead of that being the end, my speech that day was the beginning. And instead of closing their eyes, the fire service said, "Show us. Show us how."

A few days after this talk, I was telling Carl all of this incredulously, and he said something that would change both of our lives: "Have you ever thought about putting it online?"

"That would be amazing, but I have no idea how to do that."

He smiled.

"I do."

Three days later, we signed On the Job and Off, LLC, into existence. I began to work on what would be our very first online class. We called it "Capturing the Load," which is a term in technical rescue that refers to lifting a heavy object—you use rigging (ropes and hardware) to "capture the load" in order to stabilize or move it. This felt like a perfect metaphor for how to stabilize yourself and find good support systems while working on overcoming a heavy or difficult experience. Filming the course videos with the assistance of Carl and Forrest will forever be one of the most exciting moments of my life. I decided to integrate parts of my story into "Capturing the Load," feeling that it was the right way to reframe my story going forward. I wasn't done telling my story after all; I just needed to find a new avenue. On the Job and Off provided that opportunity.

Almost immediately, we found a partner in the National Volunteer Fire Council, who paid to put a thousand first responders nationwide through our first course. Their feedback gave us what we needed to grow the company and create new trainings. On the Job and Off now serves first responders in every state and Canada and provides the resources I've created to thousands and thousands of people.

Since I first starting sharing my story, I'd felt incredible relief when I realized that what happened to me hadn't happened to just me. But that relief very quickly turned to rage when I realized that what happened to me hadn't happened to just me. Every single time I stepped off a stage, handfuls of women would come up to me and tell me their stories. Stories written on napkins were pressed into my hand as I walked to the bathroom, and I have found notes tucked into my purse. It's the silent stare women give me because they are not yet safe enough to tell their stories. It's in the social media messages I get every single week. It's been a cacophony of "me too," of "our stories are really similar," of "thank you for telling the truth that I can't tell, not if I want to keep my job."

Every time I stand onstage, I bring my sixteen-year-old self with me. She couldn't speak up back then, but I sure as hell can now. I get up to show that we can tell a hard truth and the world will continue to spin. It's not

about speaking from a place of anger; it's about deciding that telling our stories matters, especially when ones
like ours aren't told often. Telling my story comes from
a place of forgiveness toward those who perpetrated
abuse, not for them or to dismiss their accountability
but to set me free. When I experienced the sexual assault
in that firehouse all those years ago, I immediately knew
I didn't have what I needed to actually bring charges
against anyone. The justice system doesn't often work
for us—for survivors. It is often at best a dismissive
witness and at worst an active perpetuator of trauma
and an enabler of abuse. So I created my own form of
justice. It didn't come in a courtroom or on behalf
of a judge or jury, but I got it. I didn't want it for one
firehouse or two or any one person in particular. I
wanted justice for the whole thing. All of them. Every
firehouse. Every comment. Every assault. Every man
who says they'll never work for or with a woman.
Every time I stand on a stage and tell my story, that is
my justice.

If I've done my job as a storyteller, I hope you'll
remember my name. I hope you will think of sixteen-year-
old Ali the next time you hear a rape joke or hear
someone question the validity of a survivor's story and
decide to take action in a way that doesn't add another
brick to the pyramid. That's why I do it. Telling my story
takes these concepts like sexual harassment and assault
out of the theoretical and puts a face on them. My face.

If you are feeling the urge to apologize for what happened to me, as so many do, as much as I appreciate the sentiment, I want you to take that feeling and stand up for the female firefighter at your station who is just trying to do her damn job. Pause the boardroom conversation to give the woman who was just spoken over time to finish her thought. Think critically about the ways you might be participating in the culture that values women as less—less worthy of respect, of opportunities, of safety. Be humble enough to look at your own life and consider the ways you have consciously or unconsciously added bricks to the pyramid. An apology or promise to do better is a good start, but it means nothing if action doesn't follow it.

I hope you'll ask yourself questions like the following ones:

Have I ever laughed at a sexist joke or comment, taken credit for a woman's work, or purposefully spoken over her?

Have I ever known a friend was getting a woman drunk for the purpose of trying to have sex with her? If I didn't act, why not? What would I do differently now?

Am I making sure women have equal opportunities to succeed in my professional life?

Do I have different expectations of my daughters than my sons?

After a talk in the fall of 2018, a woman excitedly came up to me and introduced herself as the content director for TEDxPSU, an independently organized TED Talk held at Penn State University. She told me that the lineup for their February event was already solidified, but asked if I would be interested in being added to the lineup. Back when *Where Hope Lives* had been published, I submitted my own name numerous times on the TED Talk website, doing everything I could think of to make myself seem worthy of that stage. The opportunity came exactly when it was meant to, through no direct effort of mine.

I wrote my TED Talk by hand, the words flowing freely and purposefully, fitting together like perfect puzzle pieces. But on the day, just a few hours before we were to arrive at the auditorium, panic gripped me, and those words became elusive all of a sudden. The feeling of *you aren't allowed to speak of this here* gripped me. I began to full-on panic, staring at myself in the bathroom mirror, wondering if this was the day my speaking career was going to end because I was going to get onstage and forget every word I meant to say.

Forrest put his arms around me and got serious: "Ali. There is not a doubt in my mind that you can do this. Take a breath. You know this. You can do this."

When it was time, I stepped out onstage and took my place on the red carpet dot. In the YouTube video, I can see my face relax as I begin to speak. I was aware of cameras to the left offstage and in front of me; their red lights showed me that they were recording and livestreaming.

I spoke the words "Resilience is an act of rebellion" out loud. Speaking of rebellion always makes me feel like Katniss from *The Hunger Games*, and I figured I could use a little encouragement while up on that stage. I've been asked, "What does that phrase mean?" and for me, it means that we are constantly being told what boxes we have to fit into. Societal and family expectations tell us who we "should" be. Standing up means rebelling against those expectations. And whenever we feel sunk, we must rebel against those self-sabotaging thoughts that keep us from true resilience.

To me, resilience means actively letting go of the feelings that made me sink. It means letting go of the anger I'd had toward myself, forgiving that younger part of me but keeping the anger directed at the system that harmed me and those in it who perpetuate it. I had to forgive myself but not forget. Jude Ellison S. Doyle wrote a powerful piece in response to the film *Promising Young Woman* and speaks some truths about rage: "We cannot all immolate ourselves on the pyre of our trauma; that only does the abusers' work for them. Nor will violence provide the clean, easy healing it promises. What we can do is listen to the rage; honor it, speak it, tell its story without censorship. Rage is a messenger with valuable news, if you'll stop to hear it. It is not saying that your abuser deserves to die. It's saying that you deserve to live. And look: Here you are."

Stay angry. Your anger isn't working against you; it's informing you.

A podcast production company from New York was looking to interview a female firefighter on her experiences with sexism. I was going to be interviewed by a celebrity and was so excited to find out who. While we arranged the logistics, I asked the producer if they'd like to vet my story. I connected the producers with Matt, who'd been one of my best friends all through high school, and he corroborated the things he knew happened.

There was one person from my first firehouse who I felt OK reaching out to. It was a pretty big ask, especially all those years later. *Hi, remember me? I know I unintentionally blew things up in the firehouse where we knew each other before. No big deal, but would you be willing to think back to that super fun and happy time and then talk to a complete stranger about it?* He'd been on the periphery during those tough years, generally aware of what was going on. I knew I'd alluded to him about the sexual assault.

"I'm happy to verify that info," he told me through Facebook Messenger. "Your story needs to be told over and over again until it enacts change."

As grateful as I was for his willingness, I couldn't help but wonder what would have happened if I hadn't told him or anyone else. What if I'd done what would have protected me further—what society tells me to do—and kept it a secret? What if I'd understandably buried the story so far away and never told anyone until more than a decade later? The story wouldn't be any less true, but it would be a story that people could dismiss with "Well, you didn't tell anyone at the time, so you must be making up now."

I thought to contact the detective I'd made the police report to right after I'd gotten married. I was disappointed to find out that he'd retired but was given the phone number for the detective who'd taken over his cases. The next day, I talked to this man and, upon hearing his voice, remembered a kind police officer I'd seen at incident scenes in the past.

"I heard some of your story from my colleague. I was happy you'd come in to make a report. Also, I've read your book. I believed it then and I believe you now," he told me. Tears welled up in my eyes.

After confirming all the logistics with the podcast production company, I sat writing what would become this book in a bustling Starbucks on Spring Street in Lower Manhattan as I excitedly awaited the designated time to walk around the corner to the recording studio where I was to be interviewed by Padma Lakshmi for a Spotify podcast called *Noisemakers*. Padma was kind and empathetic, and I shared with her how much I appreciated her willingness to share her own sexual assault survival story. We sat across from each other in the dimly lit recording studio, long microphone arms slightly obscuring my view of her.

In the interview, Padma asked me what I would say to other women, and I gave an answer that sometimes surprises people. I think people expect me to say, "You have to hang in there, you have to fight, stand up to those who don't believe in you . . ." and while all of that can be true, we also have to be brave enough to say, "Enough is enough." Society gives us messages like "Never give up" and "Don't let them win." That's good advice, to a point. We cannot stay in environments that do not deserve us or that are actively hurting us to prove a point. No matter how important that point might be, it isn't more important than your own well-being. Forgiving and moving forward with your life, doesn't mean forgetting what happened to you. It simply means stepping out from under the burden of pain and deciding what sort of meaning you want to make from the events.

As that year drew to a close, I was in Clearwater, Florida, speaking for the International Association of Fire Chiefs. Over eight hundred people sat in chairs, waiting for me to begin. I stood in the back of the massive conference room as I was being introduced. Conference rooms are eternally freezing, so I had my hands wrapped around the Starbucks cup that sat on the high-top table in front of me. I thought about all the days

I spent behind the counter at Starbucks, watching the businesswomen come in and out. I longed to be one of them—a woman with a place to be where she was making changes in the world. I was thinking back to that time when I heard "Please join me in welcoming Ali Rothrock!"

I walked up to the podium through the clapping crowd, confident, feeling the calm of my purpose take over. I spoke honestly and from the heart like I always do. I wore an orange and navy striped dress that I'd worn at some of my first talks, where the audiences were the smallest. After ninety minutes, I thanked them for listening and for allowing me the space to share and to no longer be alone with my story. When I finished speaking, I paused and waited for the applause to die down. Suddenly, the audience was on its feet, smiling and applauding, some people with hands up over their heads. I had the same thought I always do when receiving a standing ovation: for the longest time, no one would stand up for me. And now, look.

After stepping offstage, I stood at a table in the back of the room and spoke with a few dozen people during the break. Business cards were exchanged, and I made sure to write down a few words on the back of each of what the person wanted me to follow up with them about. I gathered up the business cards as the group thinned and counted how many of my own I had left.

My fingers brushed against a heavy gold challenge coin in a plastic case that I didn't notice someone had placed on the table next to me.

On one side, it read "Ephesians 6:11–18" and beautifully depicted each verse of the Scripture that had meant so much to me all those years ago. To this day, I still have no idea who left it there for me. It is the fourth talisman I carry in my speaker bag to each and every talk. In that speaker bag—among the HDMI adaptor, slide advancer, extra batteries, and Tide to Go stain sticks—are a few tokens. There is the Mockingjay pin that Forrest gave me on our very first Valentine's Day, accompanied by a note about how Katniss and I share the same bravery and ability to effect real, actual change. Next, there is the silver coin that was pressed into my hand many years ago by a woman who couldn't speak past her tears. I had been finishing a conversation with someone standing to the right of me when I felt movement on my left side and something being pressed into my hand. The coin has a kneeling, praying angel wrapped in wings and a halo on the front. On the back is a prayer for protection. She was already walking away when I looked up from the coin. I call it the "Survivor's Coin" because even though she didn't speak any words, I still heard her story. I also have a Saint Florian coin, Saint Florian being the patron saint of firefighters.

Several hours later, after the standing ovation, I was having a drink with the conference organizers. One man told me he'd just heard about something that had happened as soon as my talk ended. Some firefighters in the audience had noticed an older gentleman sitting near them who hadn't stood during the ovation and was still seated as the crowd left for lunch. They asked if he was OK. He exploded in an angry burst of energy he'd apparently been holding in for the entire ninety minutes I'd been talking: "*Fucking women. They think they own the goddamn world.*"

The firefighters were stunned. They walked away from him and went right up to the conference organizer I would later have drinks with. All were furious. What stood out to me about this situation was not this man's misogynistic outburst—there will be men like him for the rest of time. Being sexist is boring and disappointing but rarely surprising. What stands out to me about this is that in that audience, this man's reaction was the outlier, and the firefighters who heard it were surprised and outraged enough to tell the organizer. This shows the forward progress that the fire service has made, and I hold this example close to my heart. Forgiving but not forgetting means you acknowledge those who cling to an outdated system but you still hold people accountable for beliefs that cause harm.

Twenty years earlier, on Christmas Eve 1999, my dad decided to climb the massive pine tree in the front yard to place a large, 3D PVC star wrapped in Christmas lights. You can see it all around the town, lit from the night of Thanksgiving until New Year's. My parents can see the most magnificent sunsets from their front yard, looking east down the valley. That night as my parents readied dinner, I kept stepping outside to see the stunning colors as they blended across the sky and the star shining brightly. Streaks of cotton candy pink and robin's egg blue, fiery orange and burnt yellow. I stepped outside right before nightfall to witness one of the most stunning sunsets I'd ever seen. I stayed out in the cold, not wanting to turn away, watching my breath puff little clouds in front of me, snapping pictures as the colors in the sky bled. I felt all the time that had passed since I first walked up that driveway after becoming a fire-fighter, all the times I flew down it to get to a call, all the times I walked back up full of heartbreak. That sunset felt significant. I felt that this sunset promised peace and full closure. It promised a brand-new beginning.

A few minutes later, Mom and I sat down to dinner. Dad almost joined us but then walked back toward his office and the other bedrooms down the hall. A few moments later, he called out with a hint of concern: "Hey, Al, come back here."

Mom and I looked at each other, then got up from our chairs.

"Ali!" he called again, panic rising in his voice.

I hurriedly turned the corner into his office to find a smoky haze and pungent odor of something burning.

"Oh shit," I whispered. I touched the stereo, the wall behind the light switches, the lamps. Nothing was hot but the smell and haze were getting worse.

"I'm calling," I said, turning out of the room. I took my phone out of my back pocket and dialed, knowing exactly what that meant and who was going to come.

"9-1-1, where is your emergency?"

I told the dispatcher my parents' address, my phone number, and my name. I heard her keyboard clicking in the background.

"OK. What's going on there?"

"There's the smell of something burning..." I paused for half a second, knowing that the next piece of information was the difference between the call being dispatched as an "inside investigation" or a "dwelling fire" (an inside investigation meaning a probably boring call versus a more exciting likely fire). I really didn't want fire trucks screaming into the neighborhood on Christmas Eve, but I looked at the hazy room and sighed. "And there's a smoky haze."

"Got it. Get everyone out of the house now. I've got people on the way." *Click.*

I pulled up the scanner app, found the right county, and waited. I heard the tones drop—the tones that used to signal the start of a race for me. The tones that were once mine. The firefighters from my first firehouse were coming.

Just a few minutes later, fire trucks pulled up. I saw familiar faces get out of the trucks and hurry up our driveway, carrying big, silver, pressurized water cans and TICs (thermal imaging cameras) to see if there was heat behind the walls. I had no idea who was going to be walking through the front door. I had no control over it and started to feel uncomfortable. My mom saw the look on my face and said, "We can watch from the garage for a while."

As we stood in the dark and watched the activity, I was overwhelmed with love and gratitude for the volunteer fire service—people who do this dangerous, taxing, traumatic, time-consuming job for no money. They dropped everything, stepping away from Christmas Eve with their families to come and help mine. It's the purest form of service. I took a scan of all the faces waiting outside on the street and saw someone I felt the urge to say hi to.

Christmas is my favorite time of year, and I like to dress as obnoxiously festive as possible. That evening, I was wearing candy cane leggings, Christmas ornament earrings, and a fuzzy white sweater with a big, sequined reindeer on it. As I stepped outside, it felt like the fire trucks were shining directly on me as the sequins on my sweater reflected the flashing lights. I stood there for a moment as everyone turned to look. It wasn't more than five seconds of stillness, but it felt like a lifetime.

After talking with my firefighter friend for a bit and answering the "So what are you up to?" question, I hurried back up the driveway. I passed the firefighters who were standing in the hallway, rifled through my suitcase, and grabbed a business card. I went back outside and produced it. I saw this man look at the Maltese cross (the fire service symbol) and the company name. My title—founder and CEO. He smiled, approving. He tucked it in his front coat pocket next to his squawking radio. I looked around and saw some of those same faces from my very first fire call—the faces who held my trauma for the longest time, the faces I used to be so very afraid of. I smiled at all of them. Some smiled back; some didn't. Their response makes no difference to me anymore. I thought of us standing in our firehouse after my first call. I thought of the little girl who lay on the stretcher with blood on her face. I thought of the company I created in response to the experiences we'd had together.

"I did this for you," I thought to all of them. "For us."

And in that moment, that little girl I sent away all those years ago came out of her hiding place and came home.

I used to think forgiving meant forgetting, but over time, I decided that forgiving actually means putting down the end of the rope that ties you to the person or people who hurt you. It means your story doesn't include them anymore. This act of forgiveness is not for them but for you, and it opens up the part of your brain that is holding on to the pain, freeing it to do other things. It doesn't mean that your hurt didn't happen, it doesn't mean you aren't angry, and it doesn't mean that people are not at fault. You can have sympathy for those who hurt you and still want nothing to do with them. You can be grateful for the lessons you learned and not grateful for the harm caused. You can drop the rope that ties you without informing the person of your decision. Dropping the rope means that just because they were a part of hurting you, they don't have to be a part of your life any further. It is the ultimate act of taking your power back. Drop the rope.

During one shift on the domestic violence hotline, my phone rang around 2 a.m. I pulled on my robe and made my way down the hallway to my office. The woman on the phone softly seethed: "I hate him. I hate him every minute of my life. I can't stop hating him, even though he's gone. It's like he's still here."

"How does that hate feel?" I asked, sitting down at my desk.

She paused. "Heavy."

"I bet," I agreed. "Someday, when you're ready, you will find yourself putting down the weight. Not for him, but for you. It might not even be a very intentional thought. Just during one of those moments of hating him, you will decide that you're ready to spend that energy on something else."

REFLECTION AND ACTION

Truth #8 for Overcoming:
Forgiving Doesn't Mean Forgetting

Practice dropping the rope. Write a letter to a person who hurt or disappointed you, letting them know that your story doesn't include them anymore. There is no need to actually send it to them, as just the practice of writing it down can be powerful enough.

9

TELL HARD TRUTHS

i am not a victim of my life, what i went through
     pulled a warrior out of me
it is my greatest honor to be her.

—*Rupi Kaur*

One early morning in March 2020, my phone rang. Groggy, I looked at the caller and was instantly awake as I sat up and answered it. Forrest was awake too, his hand on my back, questioning. Our CISM team leader Mike, a dispatcher by trade, was on the other end, telling me that a firefighter had just died on the scene of a house fire.

"The scene is still active, firefighters are still there, and so is his body. Our team is being activated."

He said he'd text me the address and asked me to let him know when I was getting on the road. *Click.* I love dispatchers. They don't mess around on the phone. They are great at telling you what you need to know and then they just let you get to it.

"A firefighter just died," I said to Forrest through the dark. "I have to go."

We sprung out of bed at the same time. Forrest hurried downstairs as I flipped on the lights and pulled layers upon layers out from my closet. Downstairs, I looked into the kitchen and saw Forrest shoving bananas, apples, trail mix, and a peanut butter sandwich into a lunch box. He poured freshly brewed coffee into a thermos and, with a kiss, ushered me out the door. As soon as I got in the car, Mike texted me the address of the firehouse and told me to head there instead of going to the scene because that's where everyone was gathering.

A line-of-duty death is every single firefighter's worst possible fear realized. It's a reality we all understand is possible, but most of the time, even in the closest of calls, everyone usually returns home in one piece. I thought of what I wanted to say to people who had just seen their friend die, knowing nothing I could say would bring him back. My role wasn't to talk a lot, unlike when I'm delivering a presentation on similar topics. I was there to be someone who was removed enough to stay outside of the emotion of the incident, yet be someone who deeply knows and loves the fire service. I was also there as someone who understands the significance of line-of-duty deaths and the reverence they are to be treated with. No one knew me at this station, and I understood that I was about to be a guest in the home of people who were grieving a traumatic and sudden death.

Shock, grief, and disbelief met me as I walked in the door. Without getting in the way, I got up to speed as much as possible with the logistics of what exactly had happened on the scene. I'm only going to share what information has been made public, as the additional details and stories are not mine to tell.

Upon dispatch the night of the fire, the house had already been fully engulfed in flames. One person, the husband, made his way out, and another person, his wife, plus their dog, was still trapped. The firefighter who was killed arrived on the very first engine and had been stretching a line up near the house when the porch roof collapsed, instantly burying him under heavy, burning timber. The firefighters on scene and others got to him as fast as they could, using hose lines to keep him from burning and every rescue tool imaginable to free him. When they were finally able to rescue him, they began CPR immediately, but he was already gone. Later, the coroner's cause of death would state "Asphyxiation, smoke inhalation, and thermal burns."

I walked in circles around the station for the next few hours, gently pausing conversations to check in and standing in a place where I could be easily found if anyone wanted to talk to me one-on-one. Many did. I helped them name their feelings, encouraged them not to judge their reactions or emotions, and promised them that they would have support from our entire team for the duration of their loss.

The first COVID-19 restrictions on gatherings were put in place that week. The funeral was a few days later. Outside, a massive flag was strung up between two ladder trucks. The fallen firefighter's friends loaded his casket into the back of the last fire engine he ever rode on. The morning of the fire, as he lay under the roof and his friends desperately tried to free him from underneath the heavy timber, a helicopter landed to fly him to trauma doctors as soon as he was free. But he was pronounced dead, and the helicopter took off without him in it. On the day of his funeral, I watched a helicopter circle overhead before it hovered and bowed to his casket. A fitting and tragically perfect send-off. I continued to check in with those firefighters, gauging how they were recovering, asking each one the same two questions that told me everything I needed to know: How are you sleeping? How is your appetite? Our bodies are so wise and begin to pull energy from things like sleeping and eating when that energy is suddenly needed elsewhere.

In what ways does your body hold stress? Where do you feel it? I hold it in my stomach and shoulders. Since trauma is felt and experienced, the act of relieving that tension must be felt and experienced too. I like to use a mindfulness practice for just ten or twenty minutes to help my body process any tension before I begin my day.

Researcher Ellen Langer defines mindfulness this way: "Mindfulness is the process of actively noticing new things. It makes you more sensitive to context and engagement. When you do that, it puts you in the present. . . . It's energy-begetting, not energy-consuming. . . . I've been studying this for nearly 40 years, and for almost any measure, we find that mindfulness generates a more positive result."

When it comes to trauma and stress, chronic stress can literally change the way our brains functions and looks. The hippocampus, the part of our brains covered in receptors for stress hormones, is physically smaller in the brains of people dealing with struggles like PTSD or severe depression. But just like David Eagleman said in *Livewired*, the way our brains is formed and functioning today is not the way it will be formed and functioning tomorrow. Due to the brain's abundant ability to change, neuroscientists have shown that we can have a positive impact on our own brain function. Beginning your day by sitting quietly for two minutes, just focusing on your breath, can begin to profoundly change your response to the world. Sometimes trauma makes us not feel safe in our bodies, and this makes things like mindfulness or yoga stress-inducing or even outright triggering. You can come home to your body through patience and assistance from a trauma-informed therapist.

Part of telling the hard truth means being honest with those I work with about what their recovery journey might look like. Trauma provides a shock to our systems, a disruption of our daily lives, a deviation from what we thought our life stories were going to be. In some cases, I am with people in the first hour after a traumatic event, and sometimes they are hoping for someone to tell them that tomorrow they won't feel what they are feeling, that they can "go back to normal." Just like the brand-new survivor who was raped at the frat party who wanted to leave the hospital so it all could "be over." She was understandably desperate to want to forget what had happened to her. Trauma recovery is a long road, but it's one we don't have to walk alone.

Shortly after arriving at the station the morning the firefighter was killed, I was talking with a young firefighter who been in very close proximity to the fire-fighter as he lay dying. I thought about what our society teaches men about what it means to show compassion or sadness—that it is seen as at odds with masculinity. The aversion to acknowledging or expressing emotion is ingrained and reinforced to the point where when I asked him to name what he was feeling, he told me he didn't know how to: "I've never done that before. I don't know what you mean."

Somewhere along the way, I stopped seeing men as The Problem and started seeing them as a needed part of the solution. This mental shift occurred when I real-ized that men can be caged by gender stereotypes too and that our liberation from this restrictive culture is inextricably tied. I had a powerful experience reading Liz Plank's brilliant book on this, as her international work and research gave me the words for this revelation. In *For the Love of Men*, Liz tells us, "The biggest lie is that the fight to address male suffering is separate or at odds with the battle to liberate women. We all experience gender. We are all limited by oppressive gender stereotypes." I thought about the conversation I'd had with a paramedic who'd responded to a mass shooting, being the only paramedic on the scene for almost an hour tasked with treating ten little girls who'd all had been shot. He told me, "If I would have had the understanding that men can cry, I don't think I would have lost everything, including myself, after that incident."

I'd been taking my time with a highly requested course that I called "The Way Forward: Ending Sexual Harassment and Sexual Violence in the Emergency Services." I needed to walk the usual line while talking about divisive topics, but putting something online felt entirely different from speaking, personally, to a room full of people. It needed to be to-the-point but not so to-the-point that people stopped hearing me. After months of staring and stressing at the empty Google Docs file, I ended up with this for part of the intro:

> There are other courses that aim to address and prevent sexual harassment in the emergency ser-vices. But the ones I've seen are sanitized and

oversimplified. They talk around the cultural issues for fear of hurting people's feelings, and they do not address the systemic and institutionalized factors that allow sexual harassment and sexual violence to thrive. In this course, we are going to directly address the issues with the goal of making the emergency services safer for everyone. If you've always felt at home and welcome in the emergency services, you might think there is no way the perspectives in this course can be correct. But in order to make positive change, we need to be able to talk about these things openly and honestly. If you want to understand why you don't have more women in your ranks, or why women join and don't last long; if you want to be a more understanding, empathetic, and trauma-informed leader; and if you want to understand the culture of your station better and improve it for everyone, guys and girls, this course is for you.

I knew that some who took the course would scoff at the truth of my story, would jump to defend, and would question what I was saying. But I learned a long time ago that people's reactions to my story do not change its validity or its value. The same goes for yours. We worry about what our truth will mean to other people or if our story will challenge the way others see facets of our society or institutions we all rely on. For a while in the beginning, I kept my story to myself because I didn't know how to fit my experience in with the goodness of the fire service. I didn't want to be known as the Girl Who Hates Firefighters, which is very reductive and also just not true. I didn't want people to fear firefighters in their hometown. So I shouldered the truth on my own, thinking it was better to keep it to myself.

That week, Forrest and I stood at a retirement party for one of my police officer friends. His wife stood in front of me, swirling the ice around in her condensing glass. The man standing next to her had just mocked me for saying that I wasn't a man, so the term *fireman* didn't really apply.

"I'm so sick of the Me Too movement," she stated, trying to further antagonize.

"Why?" I asked as others stopped their conversations to listen.

"I'm just so tired of all these women complaining. Either make changes or stop talking about it."

"This is how change happens," I said. "One story at a time."

She rolled her eyes.

I'll never be sick of #MeToo. It is a reckoning, an answered prayer, a light at the end of a very long tunnel. It is not a random series of women telling lies to "get attention." It is a ripple effect of bravery, a boomerang of courage ricocheting to everyone who has a story they deserve to tell. I will listen to every hard truth told out loud. I will bear witness to every hard truth whispered in secret.

In a 2010 *HuffPost* article, Rachael Freed eloquently stated, "Telling our stories is not an end in itself, but an attempt to release ourselves from them, to evolve and grow beyond them. We tell our stories to transform ourselves; to learn about our history and tell our experiences to transcend them; to use our stories to make a difference in our world; to broaden our perspective to see further than normal; to act beyond a story that may have imprisoned or enslaved us; to live more of our spiritual and earthly potential."

We can hold conflicting emotions about the hard truth we have to tell, and they can all be correct. My experiences can be true, *and* firefighters can still be my favorite group of people. The vast majority of them are the epitome of selfless courage and humble bravery, and they are a group I am consistently proud to stand among. But I cannot and absolutely will not pretend that what happened to me did not happen. I will not downplay it, I will not lie, and I will not make this truth easier to hear. The truth is, the truth *is the truth*, and even the ugliest of truths need to be told. There are some women firefighters who are adamant about telling me that they've never experienced negative treatment in a fire station—as if I'm going to tell them that because I have, they must have—as if that's not the greatest thing for me to hear.

I used to think that if I felt anger or even rage at my past experiences, that meant I hadn't overcome them. I thought it meant I hadn't dropped the rope. But that's not the purpose anger serves. Anger and violence are not the same and, in my case, feeling anger means I've refused to let what happened to me become normalized. It never should have happened. There were so many adults in these firehouses who could have intervened, but acknowledging it meant they'd have to take an action, to choose a side, to stand up, and they were never going to. That makes me angry, still.

Kelly's anger kept her alive that day. It kept her fighting. Anger had its place in her story, and it has its place in mine. But I can feel anger *and* be whole. Both can be true. I am angry that my dreams were nightmares for so long, that every couple of nights I would wake up with my skin hot, breath panicked, blood pounding through my veins. I am angry that the term *feminist* is so polarizing and that the idea of gender equity is so incredibly divisive. I am angry that for every woman and man coming forward in the name of #MeToo, there are a dozen more saying we are liars, asking why we took so long to come forward, wondering what we hope to gain.

I am angry that safety and danger at first look the same, that an environment can be full of good people or can have its axis centered on dangerous oppression, and at first, you can't tell. I am angry that some men will only view women's worth based on what she can give them or how attractive they find her.

At my first firehouse, the truth my voice wanted to speak was viewed as a weapon. In our society, we hate truth-tellers. We reject them, cancel them, ruin them. When we hear a truth that's ugly, a truth that might require action, a truth that could upset a system that works for many but not all, we convince ourselves to hate the truth-teller instead of hating the truth.

I'm angry that standing up and telling the truth has negative ripples for the people I love. Sometimes I wish my loved ones and I could exist in a world separate from my story. But telling my hard truth means I have to be the person out in the world who has said and written words others see as the beginning of an argument. I have to be the person out there answering personal questions, defending myself over hot dogs at a Fourth of July pool party, standing up for myself at a Friendsgiving dinner. Being vulnerable onstage in an auditorium full of people is easier than doing so one-on-one. Sometimes it makes me want to be quiet, but I promised myself that my life would never again include hiding.

I have created a space where I literally stand up and ask people to listen—listen to what this job that we all love can be for some of us—then I ask them to think about what they are going to take away from this. I have officers come up afterward and ask what to do, what to say. That's why I created "The Way Forward" for On the Job and Off's training platform. A firefighter from Wisconsin commented this after taking the course: "This story is completely outlandish. . . . You are saying that if I haven't been raped I must be a raper." (Rapist?) When prompted with the "What would you change about this class?" question, he answered, "The instructor." That made me laugh.

It does sound outlandish, doesn't it? It sounds absolutely unbelievable that something like this would happen "in this day and age," as people often say. I understand that many people's life experiences preclude them from being able to believe that what I'm saying is true. If you've never experienced sexism, for example, you might think experiencing it was based on that individual instead of looking at the whole dysfunctional puzzle that contributed. It seems unbelievable that the system would fail so completely. It must be me, right? I must be complicit in some way or at least exaggerating. It must not be true because if it is true, if what I am saying actually happened the way I've been saying it did for the last decade and a half, then that means the system is unbelievably broken. That means bad things happen to good people. That means you can do nothing wrong and still be hurt. That means that many people can see something bad happening and not stop it or stand up, that people will often just blame the victim because it's easier. That's a hard truth to look in the eye.

Another piece of feedback on "The Way Forward": "This course is good if you believe all men are rapists."

I don't, obviously. But even if we as individuals are not sexist, the societal system we work within is, which means we have to be actively working to change it. Otherwise, our inaction accomplishes the same goal as those who are actively sexist—nothing changes for those the system was not designed for. To put it another way, while all men are not rapists or actively sexist, passive, casual sexism or ignoring sexism can still be as incredibly detrimental as violent sexism.

We can't just blindly call for diversity without acknowledging the barriers that exist and without an understanding of the ways that class, race, sexuality, and more intersect to further oppress. We have to be willing to look at these hard truths if we ever want to stop producing #MeToo stories.

Once, in Massachusetts, a woman came up to me after hearing me speak. She approached me sheepishly and asked if I could come and share my story with her students but "leave out the firefighting part." I was confused.

"It's just..." she murmured awkwardly in my pause. "It's just that if you come and you tell your story that way, it's going to upset the firefighters in our town, and

I don't want to lose my job. I mean, I can't have you coming and talking bad about them. Can you tell your story but leave out the firefighting part?"

This brief conversation soured my mood for days. What I heard from her was that my truth is ugly. I realized that in a lot of ways, this was always my biggest fear: being made to feel ashamed because my story made people look at things they don't want to see. Back then, I still had some trepidation around telling this hard truth. I wanted to find her and shout, "Do you think I want to have this truth to tell? Do you think I asked for this story? Do you think I want this?" To that lady and to everyone else who has ever suggested, insinuated, or outright told me to quiet my hard truth, here's what I have to say.

What happened to me in firehouses changed my life in every way. It changed me as a person; it changed the way I see, feel, and react to the world. I did not ask for these experiences or cause them. In those firehouses, the metaphorical gun was already loaded. The dangerous combination of unchallenged ignorance and institutional sexism was already there. My presence just pulled the trigger. I wanted my experience to be a horrible anomaly that existed in one town, one time, and was something I'd never have to speak of again. But in my next firehouse and in the one after that, there was that same damn truth again. And I began to realize that what I continued to experience was happening to women everywhere, every day, in almost all work environments, and that I could not be quiet about it. Holding a hard truth we are too afraid to name will wear us down. Secrets embolden abusers, and they allow our systems of oppression to continue unimpeded. We need to bring them out into the light.

In early 2020, my psychology degree was wrapping up. It had been two and a half years of full-time school that culminated in an internship serving as an advocate and crisis counselor at the local children's resource center. This is a place where children who have allegedly been abused, neglected, or trafficked go to be interviewed by a trained investigator. All the relevant agencies attend the interview, including law enforcement and child protective services, so that the children only have to tell their stories one time, lowering the chances of revictimization. My role was to provide additional mental health and sexual assault resources and on-the-spot crisis counseling.

Toward the end of my internship, I assisted on a case of child abuse where the parents—the abusers—were volunteer firefighters. Their infant had been physically abused for most of his young life, and I knew, based on the doctor's report, that many of the volunteer firefighters who were friends of the family should have seen signs of the baby's obvious injuries. They must have noticed but talked themselves out of it because the abuser was also a first responder, because they didn't want to report a friend, or because they didn't know how to report.

While looking into it, I learned that only five states train firefighters to recognize signs of child abuse, and even though all licensed emergency medical services (EMS) workers and law enforcement personnel are mandated by law to report child abuse, many received one training years ago and don't remember their state's protocol or what phone number to use. Any adult in this country is a permissive reporter and can report suspected child abuse at any time (as soon as you have an identifiable child and a reason to suspect abuse, make a report based on your state's reporting guidelines). A call to 9-1-1 is always the right move if you fear for the child's immediate safety, but a report to your state's child abuse agency will trigger an investigation within a day or so after receiving it. Any report made on behalf of this child could have potentially saved him from the eventual permanently life-altering injuries he would receive.

While in and of itself this case was upsetting, it caused me to think back to other cases I'd been involved in where the abused child had also interacted with their local first responders, and no child abuse reports were ever made. It was unacceptable to me that first responders were encountering signs of child abuse and not reporting it. I remembered a detective saying to me that due to the pandemic, kids were stuck at home with their abusers. Social services that would make home visits and would ordinarily notice signs of abuse weren't doing so. Children weren't going to school to see their teachers, who are mandated reporters. But first responders are still interacting with children both in and out of their homes—they just don't know what they are looking for or what to do if they notice something.

I paced around my office after learning about this child and the proximity of first responders to him, raging, with the doctor's report of his lifelong injuries running through my mind. The anger felt productive, like it was taking me somewhere. I kept my mind open to whatever idea was forming, and then, suddenly, a light-bulb lit up in my brain. I sat down at my desk and began to write.

I'd come up with On the Job and Off's biggest initiative yet: The C.A.R.E.S. (Child Abuse Recognition and Reporting for the Emergency Services) Project. The goal of the curriculum was to educate first responders in recognizing and understanding how to report the child abuse, neglect, and trafficking that they see while working or while off-duty. This includes child abuse that happens *inside* firehouses if a station has underage fire-fighters, like mine did. Taking the course doesn't make anyone a mandated reporter if their state's laws don't already identify them as such, but I knew most first responders aren't aware of their role in the reporting process at all.

National and international fire service and social justice organizations came on board to endorse the initiative. I worked with subject matter experts and wrote a course on what child abuse, neglect, and trafficking are; what signs first responders might see in the course of doing their job; and how to report. I vetted each state's child abuse reporting phone number and created state-specific reporting flyers to be hung in stations.

I included a module on the adverse childhood experiences, or ACEs, study, which, when I learned about it, gave me the words about the impact trauma has that I had long been looking for. The lightbulb moment that kicked off the ACEs study happened by accident in 1985, when a doctor misspoke during a physical exam to a patient who was seeing him for diabetes and a weight problem. The doctor was asking his standard questions like "How much did you weigh when you were born" and "How much did you weigh when you started high school." Instead of asking "How old were you when you became sexually active," he incorrectly asked, "How much did you weigh when you became sexually active?" The patient paused and then answered, "Forty pounds." Confident that she misspoke, the doctor waited for her to correct herself, but the patient instead got quiet. "I was forty pounds," she said again. "I was four years old. It was my father." She told her hard truth. This doctor began asking all the patients in his obesity clinic if they had a history of childhood sexual abuse. Out of 186 clients, nearly half said yes. This insight led to the ACEs study.

The original study was one of the largest ever investigations of how childhood abuse, neglect, and household challenges affect later-life health and well-being. It was conducted between 1995 and 1997 with seventeen thousand clients who agreed to answer a survey during their physical examinations with the doctor. The first research results were published in 1998, followed by more than seventy other publications through 2015. They showed the following:

1. Childhood trauma was *very* common, even in employed, middle-class, college-educated people.
2. There was a direct link between childhood trauma and the adult onset of chronic disease.
3. More types of trauma increased the risk of health, social, and emotional problems.
4. People usually experienced more than one type of trauma—that is, rarely was it only sexual abuse or only verbal abuse.

The ACEs study confirmed what many had long known anecdotally and showed a stunning link between childhood trauma and a variety of chronic diseases people develop as adults. About 61 percent of adults surveyed across twenty-five states reported that they had experienced at least one type of ACE, and nearly one in six reported that they had experienced four or more types of ACEs. An astounding 87 percent of those original seventeen thousand surveyed had experienced more than one type of trauma in their homes before they turned eighteen.

To quote Dr. Nadine Burke Harris, the current California surgeon general, who has an informative TED Talk on ACES, "Twenty years of medical research has shown that childhood adversity literally gets under our skin, changing people in ways that can endure in their bodies for decades." Not all children who are abused have severe reactions, but understandably, many do. Usually the younger the child, the longer the abuse continues, and the closer the child's relationship with the abuser, the more serious the physical and mental health effects will be. Emotional and psychological abuse and neglect deny the child the tools needed to cope with stress and learn new skills to become resilient, strong, and successful.

In Dr. Burke Harris's book *The Deepest Well*, she tells us that "childhood adversity can tip a child's developmental trajectory and affect physiology. It can trigger chronic hormonal changes that can last a lifetime. It can alter the way DNA is read and how cells replicate, and it can dramatically increase the risk for heart disease, stroke, Alzheimer's, cancer, diabetes and many autoimmune diseases, as well as depression and suicide." Experiencing child abuse or neglect can impact someone for the rest of their life, but taking action to help a child could be the moment that their life trajectory changes for the better.

With the C.A.R.E.S. Project, I was very passionate about teaching the concept of "beginning with belief." I speak about this often, referencing the "believe survivors" mantra that became well-known in and after Tarana Burke's #MeToo movement. "Beginning with belief" simply means that when we hear a story from a sexual assault survivor, we allow space in our mind for *the possibility* that they are telling the truth. Regardless of how you know their alleged perpetrator, regardless of your interactions with them, regardless of their celebrity status or role in your friend group, allow space in your brain for *the possibility* that the survivor is telling the truth. An FBI study concluded that only 8 percent of sexual assault allegations are false. Others have put the rates of false reports as low as 2 percent.

When it comes to child abuse or neglect, it's common to talk ourselves out of what we think we are noticing because of who the potential abuser is. But people who are friendly to you, respected in their communities, or have prestigious jobs can still be abusers. If your gut is telling you something is wrong, don't talk yourself out of it, and don't convince yourself that you're being dramatic. Even if you think to yourself, *Well, that person waves at me when they drive* or *They're fine to my kids*, there's no way of knowing what they're capable of behind closed doors. Abusers are great at manipulation—that's why they get away with it. Often they carefully curate a public persona that is cheerful and generous precisely so people will dismiss any abusive signs that they see. If you think, *Well, that child doesn't seem afraid of that person*, it could be because the abuse began when they were very young, so to them, it has become normalized. Sometimes on major calls, first responders see civilians who aren't crying or really reacting at all. That's because people react differently to stress and fear. How significantly they'd been impacted can't really be gauged by what emotions they're showing at the moment.

I thought about how kids like the ones whose stories I learned could maybe be helped by the C.A.R.E.S. Project, which teaches first responders what to do when they notice that something is wrong. And maybe it could help kids, like sixteen-year-old me, who find themselves surrounded by adults whose actions make them unsafe.

When we launched the C.A.R.E.S. Project in November 2020, I felt an international tidal wave of positive response and, in many ways, relief from first responders who felt like they were finally being equipped with knowledge of what to do in these situations. The pilot data I pulled from our first one hundred students was astounding. Questions answered after taking the course showed that 75 percent of first responders noted that they had seen signs of child abuse and not recognized it and 34 percent had seen signs of trafficking and had not recognized it. Ninety-five percent and 94 percent of participants said they were more confident in recognizing the signs of child abuse and trafficking, respectively, since taking the course. And most important of all, 79 percent and 75 percent of participants stated they were more likely to report signs of child abuse or trafficking, respectively. We'd accomplished the mission.

The C.A.R.E.S. Project was a bit of a mission shift for On the Job and Off, but I knew we could make it work. When our students began asking for more, I knew I needed to create a separate entity for initiatives like that one. So just one month after launching the C.A.R.E.S. Project, I announced First Responders Care, a nonprofit powered by NDRI Ventures, which holds the Center for Fire, Rescue, and EMS Health Research. First Responders Care seeks to empower first responders to take an active role in their community's resilience by offering accessible education and resources provided by a variety of diverse perspectives through an anti-oppressive, culturally sustaining, and trauma-informed approach. I assembled a powerhouse board of directors, and in January 2021, we were off to the races. I set our first goal at putting ten thousand first responders through the C.A.R.E.S. Project.

Every single day can't be spent overcoming, and every single day can't be spent telling hard truths. We need rest—mindful rest. Rest and sleep are not the same thing; rather, sleep is one of the many components of rest our minds and bodies need. In her book *Sacred Rest*, Dr. Saundra Dalton Smith tells us about the seven types of rest (physical, mental, emotional, creative, sensory, social, and spiritual). Physical rest is where sleep falls, and it can also include restorative physical activities, like yoga. Mental rest is being intentional about giving our brains breaks, like through a fifteen-minute mindfulness session. Emotional rest is huge for first responders or those in other helping professions, and it means giving ourselves time to refill our cups instead of always emptying them out for others. Creative rest is big for me, as all of my work requires a lot of creative output. Resting in this capacity could look like watching a movie that makes me feel creatively inspired. Sensory rest is needed for us all, and this could look like disconnecting from technology or using noise-canceling headphones. Social rest could look like giving ourselves space from relationships that feel draining, and spiritual rest could mean actively engaging in nature.

Telling hard truths can be very depleting and often make us feel very vulnerable, even if we're doing it for the right reasons. It's imperative to have a place to process and rest while you are on that part of your journey.

For me, a daily journaling practice is what kept my head above water for all those years, and it's a habit I still use to this day. At the time of this writing, I am on my ninety-fifth journal, having written almost every day since August 2005.

REFLECTION AND ACTION

Truth #9 for Overcoming:
Tell Hard Truths

Is there a hard truth you need to tell—one you've been keeping to yourself? Name a few safe people you can tell it to. Are there people who have publicly told a similar hard truth that you can look to? How can you prioritize rest based on the seven types Dr. Dalton Smith names?

10

RECOVERY HAS NO TIMELINE

I wrote my way out, wrote everything down far as I
  could see.
I wrote my way out.
                    —Lin-Manuel Miranda, Hamilton

In the years since my first day as a firefighter, I've learned that trauma is not always just one thing. Traumatic experiences aren't always big incidents but can be like a river against a stone, slowly wearing us down over the course of time. Dealing with constant microaggressions, overt sexism, and occasional sexual violence in the fire service wore me down until I no longer believed I could exist safely in the world. The events had ripped me apart, but they weren't enough to make the people involved do anything differently. Their apathetic inaction showed me that what happened to me did not matter and, therefore, I must not matter. The pain stripped away my autonomy and left me empty, searching.

A moment of sexual violence in a dark, nameless firehouse provided proof that my body was something to be owned, to be possessed, to be violated at the whim of someone else. My consent was never necessary. My world stopped while everyone else's kept on spinning. That feeling of literal and metaphorical suffocation would accompany every memory of the fire service, every experience, every moment of helplessness until I was able to divorce myself from the active pain and give myself grace for the fact that this trauma will always be a part of my life story.

At the bottom of my ocean, I encompassed myself into a protective chrysalis, cocooned away from the world until I was safe enough to reemerge radically different. Adversity is often the catalyst that makes the dissonant chords of our lives resolve, and I am now finally peaceful with the resolution. I am in a place where I can take stock of who I was before, during, and after trauma and be OK with it all. My body is my own again, no longer interrupted. My emotions are my own; I no longer have to question the validity of what I'm feeling. I've shed the shame, being very clear on where the blame belongs.

For a long time, I thought that my "before and after" was the day I joined the fire service, that this separation in my life was bound by big red trucks, emergencies, violence, and apathy. But that isn't it. The greatest demarcation in my life is before and after the swim for my life. Crossing this threshold is what set me free. Being out of the water didn't take away the trauma that drowned me, but it allowed me the space to breathe and make decisions for my future. My hair continued to drip, my fingers were waterlogged, my skin expelled sand. But I kept myself on the shore and took steps away from the water's edge when I felt ready.

I thought it was my love for firefighting that I was holding on to while I sunk to the bottom of my ocean. But that wasn't all that was keeping me sunk. It was my past self, the before-Ali. I knew that if I got out of the water, I might not ever find the pieces of me I sent away all that time ago. I would have to take my butterfly self, fresh from her cocoon, and continue to walk until I was able to get far enough away from the water's edge that my overcoming was secure and be okay with finding a new version of myself on the shore.

That eventual overcoming felt like the first day of spring when the thaw has finally gone out of the air and people start to turn their faces to the sun. Sometimes moments don't actually hurt anymore—it's just the memory that does. I could choose what I did with the memories. Recognizing this set me free.

In my forever favorite book, *Man's Search for Meaning*, Holocaust survivor and psychologist Viktor Frankl proved our stunning ability to choose. I am a person

who feels all of my feelings in a big way. I was truly trans-
formed when I put into practice that I too had the ability, as we all do, to step outside of my feelings and not
get swept away by them. We have the ability to choose
what we do with our feelings, never dismissing them
but understanding that we are not controlled or defined
by them.

As a new survivor from trauma, you could be running on adrenaline and shock for a while. You might
be feeling like you're all good and you're just ready to
get on with your life, but then the grief creeps in and
you start to feel the turbulence of emotions that trauma
brings. Kelly described it as "a boomerang." As I often
say, recovery isn't linear—it's cumulative. You might
feel better after putting in a lot of work, and then something happens that brings those events back. Our bodies
hold things way longer than our minds do. Those reactions don't invalidate all the work you've done—it just
means you've still got some work to do. And you can
work on restorying at any time, even decades later. I
know what it's like to want to rush your way to your
After. I know you want to make the meaning and hurry
up and heal, but these things cannot be rushed. Your life
is happening right on time.

We get to steer the boat of our lives, and even if we've
been floating aimlessly for a while, letting the waves
take us, we can always pick up a paddle and begin to
choose our direction. Realizing this helped me restore

the power of my life to me, and that broke me free from being the victim of other people. This can become so completely consuming, and it can be hard to think of ourselves as anything other than Someone Who Has Been Hurt. But we are not broken people. We are people who have responded appropriately to trauma. Our brains and bodies protected us the way they knew how to.

Post-traumatic stress disorder has an alternative: post-traumatic growth.

As my friend Dr. Anne Bisek told me in an episode of my *Over a Cup* podcast, post-traumatic growth has five factors: increased ability to relate to others, new possibilities, personal strength, spiritual change, and appreciation of life. As much as I was ever in the disorder, I am so much more established in growth.

I put my love for firefighting on the altar and returned it to God, releasing myself from it. I hoped that I would find the love again, and it has indeed roared back into me like a summer thunderstorm, fierce and consuming. Hope is not just a trendy word; it's not a fleeting, meaningless platitude. It is fire, it is rebellion, it is perseverance, it is a firm belief in better days. I could forever be the woman who had to learn to live at the bottom of her mental grave, or I could be the woman who lives every day like it's the miracle she fought for. I choose to be the latter.

A few months before I joined the fire service, when my first firehouse was a building like any other, I turned sixteen years old. Like many volunteer firehouses, this one rented out their banquet halls as a way to make money. So I had my sixteenth birthday party at that firehouse, having no idea what that building and the people in it were about to mean for my life. I rewatched the home video of that party recently, seeing my sixteen-year-old self dance around while talking to my friends. I casually passed the door that led to the engine bay, never crossing that threshold, not yet stepping into that next chapter of my life.

I think of that first firehouse now; it's just like the hundreds I've been in since. There is a bay that has since been expanded but still smells like diesel fuel and wet hose. There's a watch room with windows that allows you to see into the bay and out onto the quiet residential street. I see my sixteen-year-old self there, listening to the radio and learning box alarms. She was so certain of her purpose. In spite of what happened there and in the other stations, I believe in fire service and in a world that will no longer produce stories like mine. But until that day, I will continue to tell my story to show anyone who is listening that it is possible to walk through the fire, get burned, find beauty and purpose in the scars, embrace them, and then move forward— to show those watching that we are so much more than the things that happen to us.

Our bodies are a constellation, a collection of stories reflected back to us, an entire galaxy that we hold. I've cared for the places that held trauma, fear, and violence and have filled in those black holes with wholeness. I have a mind that I can trust, a mind that has withstood immense stress and still found room to grow, dream, and create. I have a loud voice that speaks hard truths, arms capable enough to care for other people, and an indestructible heart. My hands were powerful enough to hold on to a dream; my legs were strong enough to swim and save my life. I think of all the areas in my mind that were cut and bled, scabbed, and then scarred. The heavy scar tissue dissolved when I was resting at the bottom of my ocean, and when I stepped out of the water, I was free to take steps forward.

We are more than just the collection of stories we tell about ourselves. We are the moments of quiet courage we display, the ones that no one ever sees. They are like a sunset over an empty ocean, unwitnessed but no less real. We are both our potential and our right now, the integration of our history and future. We are our adversity—not the adversity itself, but the decisions we make right after. We are what we *choose* to be. We are perpetual new beginnings. If God is a poet, you are the poem.

REFLECTION AND ACTION

Truth #10 for Overcoming:
Recovery Has No Timeline

As much as we want to hurry toward our After, our overcoming timelines cannot be rushed. Each day counts. Acknowledge to yourself how far you have come. Make a list of at least three examples of your growth and progress. Allow yourself to celebrate these accomplishments!

When I am dust sing these words over my bones:
She was a voice.

  —*Sue Monk Kidd*, The Book of Longings

EPILOGUE

It turns out that the first firefighters I've ever known were right. I didn't belong in their firehouse. No one belongs in a space where they are made to feel small, where their boundaries are willfully violated, where every day is an exercise in gaslighting. Through their lens, they were simply protecting themselves from someone who wanted to change their world in ways that would have made it unrecognizable to them. To some of them, I was, and will forever be, wrong.

I was representative of what was coming for them in time. I was probably the first feminist they'd ever known. They gave me my #MeToo story, but instead of letting them take my voice, I found a way to magnify it. Since being denied a seat at their table, I made my own, building it carefully but deliberately over the years. It's a table that has space for anyone. Come and sit.

I don't have to stand in rooms with my back to a door anymore. I can stand in rooms full of firefighters who I don't know, who are drinking, and not feel like I need to run away. I can have conversations with people who think my existence is antagonistic to theirs and not dissociate. I can wear necklaces and not feel the squeeze of a man's fingers. I have integrated all my experiences into my life story, and I no longer have events that are blacked out like a scene in a film that won't play. I have moved beyond those memories to tell a different story, and I have gone back into that world to help create a version of it that has room for everyone.

Dear reader, I hope that the next time you see a fire truck riding down the street, you don't think of the reasons I had to walk away from the fire service. It is my deepest hope that instead, you will think of all the reasons I had to stay. I hope you think of the powerful good that exists in the vast majority of fire stations and the deep sense of service and sacrifice and bravery that lives there. I hope you'll stop by the firehouse for a visit, to meet those who will come to help you at the drop of a tone. Let your kids climb on the trucks and try on fire gear. Maybe they'll choose to become a firefighter someday. Maybe you will. (Volunteer fire companies are always accepting applications!)

Yes, all my trauma happened among firefighters. But so did my overcoming.

This empty page is dedicated to those who aren't yet able to share their stories.

ACKNOWLEDGMENTS

The words on these pages are mine, but they did not come from me alone. They were formed by all those in my life who loved and supported me during this time and those who took a chance on this story.

To my husband, Forrest. You are the best advice giver, the best listener, and the best friend I could have ever hoped for. With your encouragement, love, and support, anything is possible.

To my parents, Marc and Tracy. Dad, you tell me often that I "always have more in the tank," and whether I'm about to step on stage or meet a challenge, your words always carry me through. Mom, you showed me that women belong in all environments and conversations and that I am capable of anything I set my sights on. I am who I am because of you both.

Julia—I might be two years older than you but continue to learn from the example you set. I don't know how I got so lucky to have a sibling like you.

Hannah—Everyone always assumes we are sisters, and if family is something we get to choose, I choose you. Thank you for swimming with me. GIAP.

Carl—From you, I learned the power and nuance of storytelling. You are able to speak so eloquently about life's lessons because of all you've overcome, and I am very proud to know you. Here's to taking big swings together! *snaps*

To all the women who came before me, who endured so much so I could have strength written into my DNA. To my grandmothers, Mary Genevieve Warren (who I was fortunate enough to know) and Sally Sullivan Peterson (who I never got to meet). To all the women who have paved their own paths in big and small ways, your existence gives me peace.

To my agent, Keely. Thank you for believing in my story and for being willing to dream really big with me. I cherish your insight and friendship and am so excited to continue this journey with you.

To the entire team at Broadleaf Books. First and foremost, my editor Lisa. Your talent, perspective, and kindness made the editing process thoroughly enjoyable. To all those who had a hand in bringing this book into the world—including my production editor Claire and cover designer James—I will forever be in awe of the fact that I got to work with people who are as smart, generous, and enthusiastic as you.

NOTES

Chapter 2

41 **"Five days later, Clara Barton"**: David McCullough, *The Johnstown Flood* (Simon & Schuster, 1987) 229, 230.

47 **"In Eagleman's book *Livewired*"**: David Eagleman, *Livewired* (Pantheon, 2020) 12.

52 **"an easy forgiveness . . . a kind of cheap grace"**: Terri Jentz, "Strange Piece of Paradise by Terri Jentz (2006 Picador Books)," h0ll0wm9n, January 15, 2017, YouTube video, 11:33–38, https://www.youtube.com/watch?v=sCOiRo9K_lw.

52 **"Oh, I didn't think much about him"**: Jentz, 11:25–27.

52 **"It was tremendously detrimental"**: Jentz, 21:58–22:05.

52 **"I felt like there was some part of my being"**: Terri Jentz, *Strange Piece of Paradise* by Terri Jentz (2006 Picador Books) https://www.youtube.com/watch?v=sCOiRo9K_lw.

59 **"Shame is not just a feeling; it's a barrier to functioning"**: Liz Plank, *For the Love of Men* (New York: St. Martin's, 2019), 80.

Chapter 3

90 **"Recognize your patterns, label your thoughts and emotions, accept them, and act on your values"**: Susan David and Christina Congleton, "Emotional Agility," *Harvard Business Review*, November 2013, https://hbr.org/2013/11/emotional-agility.

112 **"Author Diane Coutu defines resilience as 'the skill'":** *On Emotional Intelligence* (Harvard Business Review Press, 2015) 115.

Chapter 7

166 **"paradigms are powerful because they create the lens through which we see the world":** Steven R. Covey, *The 7 Habits of Highly Effective People* (New York: Free Press, 2004), 32.

179 **"explains Dr. Jaime Zuckerman":** Simone M. Scully, 2020, *'Toxic Positivity' Is Real—and It's a Big Problem During the Pandemic* https://www.healthline.com/health/mental-health/toxic-positivity-during-the-pandemic#What-is-toxic-positivity?.

180 **"In her article 'How Resilience Works,' Diane Coutu":** *On Emotional Intelligence* (Harvard Business Review Press, 2015) 113.

Chapter 8

191 **"Jude Ellison S. Doyle wrote a powerful piece":** Jude Ellison S. Doyle, 2020, *Scum Manifesto: Promising Young Woman*, doyles.substack.com.https://doyles.substack.com/p/scum-manifesto-promising-young-woman.

Chapter 9

208 **"Researcher Ellen Langer defines mindfulness this way: 'Mindfulness'":** *Emotional Intelligence: Mindfulness*, (Harvard Business Review Press, 2015) 4.

211 **"In *For the Love of Men*, Liz tells us, 'The biggest lie'":** Liz Plank, *For the Love of Men* (New York: St. Martin's, 2019) 20.

225 **"'Twenty years of medical research'":** Nadine Burke Harris, *The Deepest Well* (Mariner Books, 2018) xv.

225 "childhood adversity can tip a child's developmental trajectory":
Nadine Burke Harris, *The Deepest Well* (New York: Houghton
Mifflin Harcourt, 2018), xv.

229 "seven types of rest": Saundra Dalton Smith, *Sacred Rest* (New
York: Faith Words, 2017).

RESOURCES

- On the Job and Off (www.onthejobandoff.com)
- First Responders Care (www.FRCare.org)
- National Sexual Assault Hotline: 1-800-656-4673
- National Domestic Violence Hotline:
  1-800-799-7233
- National Suicide Prevention Hotline:
  1-800-273-8255
- Women in Fire (www.womeninfire.org)

Books Mentioned

- *Where Hope Lives*, Ali W. Rothrock
  (www.aliwrothrock.com)
- *The 7 Habits of Highly Effective People*, Stephen
  Covey
- *Strange Piece of Paradise*, Terri Jentz
- *For the Love of Men*, Liz Plank
- *The Shack*, Wm. Paul Young
- *They Call Me Mr. De*, Frank DeAngelis
- *Man's Search for Meaning*, Viktor Frankl

RESOURCES

- *Home Body*, Rupi Kaur
- *Grief: The Event, the Work, the Forever*, Lynn Shiner and Lisa Zoll
- *Know My Name*, Chanel Miller
- *The Deepest Well*, Dr. Nadine Burke Harris
- *Sacred Rest*, Dr. Saundra Dalton Smith